The Consolation of Philosophy

The Consolation of Philosophy

Anicius Manlius Severinus Boethius

Translated by David R. Slavitt

HARVARD UNIVERSITY PRESS

Cambridge, Massachusetts   London, England

First Harvard University Press paperback edition, 2010

Library of Congress Cataloging-in-Publication Data

Boethius, d. 524.
[De consolatione philosophiae. English]
The consolation of philosophy / Anicius Manlius
Severinus Boethius ; translated by David R. Slavitt.
p.   cm.
Includes bibliographical references.
ISBN 978-0-674-03105-0 (cloth : alk. paper)
ISBN 978-0-674-04835-5 (pbk.)
1. Philosophy and religion.   2. Happiness.
I. Slavitt, David R., 1935–   II. Title.

B659.D472E5 2008
100—dc22   2008010051

For Jarmilla

CONTENTS

ACKNOWLEDGMENTS

Poem 3 of Book V appeared in *Per Contra* (Spring 2007), and I am grateful to its editors. I should also like to express my gratitude to the outside readers to whom the press sent the manuscript for review. They made a number of very helpful suggestions and offered corrections that I have adopted. I want to thank Seth Lerer for contributing an intelligent and useful introduction. Finally, I am deeply and always grateful to my wife for her careful proofreading and, on occasion, line editing, most of which she did on her stationary bicycle!

—David Slavitt

INTRODUCTION

Seth Lerer

The brilliant, brutally truncated life of Anicius Manlius Severinus Boethius (c. 480–524) straddled the
worlds of classical antiquity and early Christian culture. As the scion of one of Italy's most influential
aristocratic families, Boethius received an education
befitting a future imperial official. He studied Greek
and Latin classics and received his training in rhetoric, forensics, and the niceties of diplomacy. He prac-
ticed, too, the Christianity that had become the accepted religious practice of the aristocracy since the
fourth century, and his father-in-law, Symmachus,
had been one of the most powerful figures in the
doctrinal debates that rocked the Church during the
fifth century.

Of course, by the end of that century, the institu-
tions of the Roman Empire had been irrevocably
changed. The eastern end of empire had its seat in
Constantinople, and the western remains were now
governed by the Ostrogoths. The reign of Theodoric, which began in 493, incorporated the old

Roman offices as a courtesy to the surviving aristocracy. In such a world, a young man like Boethius could aspire to be a provincial governor or a ceremonial consul. It was this latter position that he attained in 510, and by 522 he had risen to the position of Master of Offices at Theodoric's court in Ravenna. Intrigue and rivalry, there as in all courts, were the currency of everyday advancement, and just a year after his appointment as Master, Boethius found himself traduced, denounced, stripped of his position, and under house arrest. The eastern and western Churches were in sharp disagreement over basic tenets of belief. Theodoric was an Arian Christian (holding a position on the relationship of God the Father to the Son that differed from what would become the mainstream, "Trinitarian" view), and his religious and political alliances were in flux during the early 520s. Relationships with the Roman pope, with the eastern emperor in Constantinople, and with the old Roman (but now Christian) aristocracy were tense. It may be no exaggeration to say that these were years of paranoia, and Theodoric was receptive to whatever rumors flew about his court. Whether Boethius really supported the Byzantines against the Goths, and whether his staunch defense of the old Roman Senate irked the emperor, his fate was sealed, and in October 524 he was imprisoned and executed in the town of Pavia, far from the seat of rule and from his family.

Like many courtiers of successive centuries, Boethius was both a politician and an intellectual. His early life was spent translating and adapting the inheritance of Greek philosophy for Latin readers. As he outlined his plan in his Commentary on Aristotle's *Perihermeneias* (probably written in his twenties):

> I shall translate into Latin every work of Aristotle's that comes into my hands, and I shall write commentaries on all of them; any subtlety of logic, any depth of moral insight, any perception of scientific truth that Aristotle has set down, I shall arrange, translate, and illuminate by the light of a commentary. And I shall also translate and comment upon all Plato's dialogues and put them into Latin form. Having completed this not unworthy project, I shall bring the thought of Aristotle and Plato somehow into harmony, and show that these two philosophers are not at odds in everything as a great many people suppose.

It matters little that the project never reached completion. What matters is that this young scholar, from the start, saw his career as one of reading and translating, understanding and interpreting. Even in partially realized form, the project made him famous among his intellectual peers. When his younger contemporary Cassiodorus wrote a letter of recommendation for him, he could praise: "In your hands, Greek teachings have become Roman doctrine."

In addition to his work in Greek philosophy, Boethius contributed to the growing debates emerging in the early Catholic Church. His four Theological Tractates carefully analyze the questions about the nature of Christ and the relationships between his humanity and divinity. Deeply indebted to Neoplatonic thought and to the writings of St. Augustine, the Tractates also work, structurally, according to the classical techniques of inner dialogue and intellectual debate. It is not so much that Boethius attempted to synthesize classical and Christian idiom or ideology. It is rather that he could adapt the forms of the Greek and Roman philosophical dialogue to matters of theological inquiry.

The Consolation of Philosophy, written while he was imprisoned, sustains many of Boethius's earlier intellectual concerns and literary aspirations. It offers a conspectus of Platonic philosophy and Aristotelian method. It develops the pedagogic dialogue found in the works of Plato, Cicero, and St. Augustine into a dramatic narrative of self-awareness. It takes the literary form of the Menippian satire—alternating poetry and prose—to create a kind of parallel dialogue between the discourses of literary and logical inquiry. And it transmutes the central myths of classical paganism to provide allegories of wandering, struggle, and reward that the prisoner and the reader may use to locate themselves in the spiritual world.

The reader coming to the *Consolation* for the first time—especially in David Slavitt's uniquely evocative translation—should not be daunted by the doctrinal debates or by the details of late antique history that shaped its making. Instead, the reader should savor the resonances of its verse: from the ruefulness of its opening meters in Book I, through the power of its natural descriptions in Book II, the purview of its cosmology in Book III, the affecting retellings of the tales of mythic heroes in Books III and IV, to the knowing serenity in Book V. These are poems deeply indebted to the lyric and dramatic forms of Roman literary history: Virgil and Ovid chime throughout; Seneca's tragic heroes and heroines break through. The reader should attend as well to the prose dialogue that frames the poems. Lady Philosophy remains one of the greatest teachers in

Western literature, especially when the prisoner remains one of the most obtuse of students. The *Consolation*'s reader should find himself or herself in the
prisoner: learning from the method of dialectical argument, moving from the avowal of opinion to the
recognition of truth.

And yet, the *Consolation* does not simply juxtapose
two forms of writing for simple contrast. Both the
poetry and prose are deeply figurative, rich with
metaphors of travel, of the home, of music, and of
craft. Both, too, are deeply allusive, bringing together
literary echoes and resonant rewritings. Homeric
and Virgilian epic, Ovidian love poetry, Senecan
tragedy all jostle in Boethius's exquisite Latin. But
this allusiveness is more than just a great scholar's
showing off. It is a principle of form, a literary
method, as Boethius makes clear that all experience
is a rereading of the past, that life is made up of the
books we have read, and that, in particular, the progress of his student-prisoner requires him to look
back over his own writings and the early sections of
this dialogue to put aside past doubts and desires
and aspire to an understanding of his true home in
the stars.

In these ways, the *Consolation* is a work of literate
and literary understanding. It is very much a work
about the place of books in culture, about life as

something of a library of the imagination. "I used to write cheerful poems," the work begins, and its first word is the Latin *carmina*. Boethius moves from a poet to a philosopher in the course of the work. But he remains grounded in the avowals of the writer's life. *Carmina qui quondam, studio florente peregi:* "These are the songs I used to sing." How can we not recall the opening of Virgil's *Aeneid,* where the poet announces, *Arma virumque cano,* "I sing of arms and of a man"?

The man of whom Boethius sings was not the founder of the Roman world but one of its last victims. His exploits are not those of discovery, love, and martial conquest but of moral growth. Much like Aeneas, the prisoner of the *Consolation* is a traveler—but his travels take him to a *patria* of spiritual understanding. His *via* is a way of reason. (Indeed, Boethius adopts the Latin phrase *via et ratio,* "way and reason," to translate the Greek word *methodos,* "method"—a word that has, in its own etymology, the sense of being on the road to understanding.) And so each book of the *Consolation* charts his journey. Book I finds the prisoner in self-pitying lament, and lady Philosophy appears before him to initiate a dialogue that will locate him securely on the path of moral understanding. Part of that understanding lies in a rejection of the wiles of Fortune, and Book II presents one of the best-known images of worldly well-being—the wheel of Fortune—to press home to the prisoner his need to reject power, wealth, and status in favor of the true good of wisdom. Book III illustrates how that wisdom has a source in the divine and that such ideals as virtue, goodness, and happiness remain inextricably linked with the divinely ordered cosmos. Books IV and V raise questions about divine knowledge and human free will, about causality and contingency, and by the *Consolation*'s end the prisoner, and ideally the reader, leaves the dialogue convinced that divine omniscience is not a barrier to human choice: that is, that God's knowledge of events, existing as it does outside linear time, does not in itself cause those events to happen.

In the course of these philosophical discussions, Philosophy offers up some of the most moving poetry of late Latin literature. The poems on the changing seasons in Book II look back over the genres of the pastoral, the georgic, and the lyric to write a story of world history as literary history. The magnificent hymn to creation in Book III (poem 9), modeled on Plato's cosmological vision in his *Timaeus,* remains one of the greatest paeans to the divine ever composed. The brilliantly allusive trio of poems on the major figures of Greek mythology—Orpheus in Book III, poem 12; Odysseus in Book IV, poem 3;

and Hercules in Book IV, poem 12—synthesizes epic subject matter with dramatic declamation. These poems are not simply masterpieces of late antique verse; they were the stimulus to a whole range of later literary imaginings, from the Old English *Meters of Boethius*, through the Old French allegories of the *Roman de la Rose*, to Chaucer's Middle English *Troilus and Criseyde*, and beyond.

This literary afterlife marks *The Consolation of Philosophy* as one of the most influential and most widely copied, translated, and commented upon works of literature in Western culture. Recovered, perhaps by Cassiodorus decades after its composition, the work made its way by the eighth and ninth centuries into the central Europe of Charlemagne and subsequently to the England of Alfred the Great. Some of the most magnificent of medieval illustrated manuscripts are those of the *Consolation*: Boethius in his study, lady Philosophy in her lettered robe, Fortune and her wheel, and the torments and adventures of the poetry's mythological figures all became the subjects of illumination. In England alone, the *Consolation* survives in translations ranging from those of King Alfred's court in the late ninth century to that of Geoffrey Chaucer at the end of the fourteenth and that of Queen Elizabeth at the end of the sixteenth. Chaucer's *Boece*, as it was known, was one of the first books printed by William Caxton when he brought the new technology of movable type to England in the mid-1470s (his edition dates from 1479), and Boethius was clearly in the mind of Sir Thomas More as he reflected on his own imprisonment in 1535. For the historian Edward Gibbon, two and a half centuries later, the *Consolation* remained "a golden book, worthy of the leisure of Plato or Tully [i.e., Cicero]."

Boethius has thus played a unique role in the history of English letters, and David Slavitt brings to the *Consolation* his own unique sensitivity to the nuances of Latin poetry and the many forms of English verse. Scholars coming to his translation will find much that sparkles and surprises: for example, in the frank colloquialisms of such moments as Book V, prose 6, when Philosophy responds to the prisoner's request to explain "the apparent randomness of good and bad fortune": "This is the great question, isn't it?" They will also find poetry restored to verses long reduced to prosaic paraphrase, as in this exquisite alliterative moment in Book III, poem 12:

> Orpheus long ago sang
> his dirge for Euridyce's death
> and rooted trees ran to hear
> and running rivers stopped
> to listen.

Passages such as this one will entice the reader new to the *Consolation,* too, as will moments in which Slavitt juxtaposes commonplace and conundrum to give life to old phrases: for example, in Book I, poem 1, where the image of the prisoner's "fair-weather friends" looks ahead to the foul storms that will beset his mind in Book II; or in Book IV, poem 3, where the Latin line *vela Neritii ducis* (literally, "the sails of the Ithacan leader") generates a phrasing evocative of the opening of Ezra Pound's *Cantos:*

> The Ithacan's black ship
> and the rest of his wandering fleet
> the winds drove to the island
> where the fair goddess dwells.

Slavitt's *Consolation* is a translation, then, that reaches back to histories of classical translation and introduces one of the great works of Western literature to new readers at the start of a new century.

Suggested Further Reading

Chadwick, Henry. *Boethius: The Consolations of Music, Logic, Theology, and Philosophy.* Oxford: Clarendon Press, 1981.
Courcelle, Pierre. *La consolation de philosophie dans la tradition littéraire.* Paris: Etudes Augustiniennes, 1967.

Gibson, Margaret, ed. *Boethius: His Life, Thought, and Influence.* Oxford: Blackwell, 1981.

Lerer, Seth. *Boethius and Dialogue: Literary Method in The Consolation of Philosophy.* Princeton: Princeton University Press, 1985.

Marenbon, John. *Boethius.* New York: Oxford University Press, 2002.

O'Daly, Gerard. *The Poetry of Boethius.* London: Duckworth, 1991.

✥ BOOK I ✥

I

I used to write cheerful poems, happy and life-
    affirming,
      but my eyes are wet with tears and the poems
        are those
that only grieving Muses would prompt me to
    compose,
      heartbreaking verse from a suffering,
        heartbroken man,
but these woeful songs turn out to be my
    consoling companions.
    Those glories of my young manhood have
      lately become
the comforts of old age that has come upon me
    too soon
      as the burdens of anguish add to those of my
        years.
My hair is prematurely gray and my skin hangs
    loose

on a poor, precarious frame. To the young,
            Death
is a threat to their pleasures, but now that I am
            worn down and out
    and it offers at last a remission of all my pains,
it is cruel, paying no heed to my imploring cries,
    and will not deign to close my weeping eyes.
In my salad days, I was rich, and whimsical
        Fortune smiled
    for a little while, but then she turned away
that faithless face of hers, and my bitter life drags
            out
        its long, unwanted days. My fair-weather
            friends
admired me, paid compliments, and envied my
            luck,
        but now they see how my foothold was always
            uncertain.

I was writing this in a silence broken only by the
scratchings of my quill as I recorded these gloomy
thoughts and tried to impose upon them a certain
form that in itself is curiously anodyne, when there
was a presence of which I gradually became aware
looming over my head, the figure of a woman whose
look filled me with awe. Her burning gaze was inde-

scribably penetrating, unlike that of anyone I have ever met, and while her complexion was as fresh and glowing as that of a girl, I realized that she was ancient and that nobody would mistake her for a creature of our time. It was impossible to estimate her height, for she seemed at first to be of ordinary measure, but then, without seeming to change, she appeared to be extraordinarily tall, so that her head all but touched the heavens. I was certain that if she had a mind to stretch her neck just a little, her face would penetrate the skies, where it would be utterly lost to human view. Her dress was a miracle of fine cloth and meticulous workmanship, and, as I later learned, she had woven it herself. But it had darkened like a smoke-blackened family statue in the atrium as if through neglect and was dingy and worn. I could see worked into the bottom border the Greek letters Π (pi—for practice) and slightly higher Θ (theta—for theory) with steps that were marked between them to form a ladder by which one might climb from the lower to the upper. Some ruffians had done violence to her elegant dress, and clearly bits of the fabric had been torn away. In her right hand she held a few books, and in her left she carried a scepter.

As she noticed the Muses of poetry surrounding my bed, helping me find the words to express my grief, her expression changed to one of anger, and with her eyes blazing she demanded, "Who let these chorus girls in here to approach a sick man's bedside? They have no cures for what ails him. Indeed, what they offer will only make his condition worse! What we want is the fruits of reason, while all they have is the useless thorns of intemperate passion. If he listens to their nonsense, he will accustom himself to depression instead of trying to find a cure." And then, addressing them directly, she spoke with even more animus: "If your dangerous foolishness were distracting some mere boor, as it generally does, I should not object so strenuously. That would have nothing to do with me. But this is an educated man, a student of Parmenides, Zeno, and Plato. You are like the Sirens, and your blandishments will lead only to his destruction. Be gone! And leave him to my Muses to care for him and heal him."

My Muses blushed, hung their heads in shame, and withdrew from the room, while my eyes filled with tears at the departure of my companions. And this woman of such commanding authority . . . Who was she? What did she have in mind for me?

She approached my bed and seated herself at the foot of it. She saw the confusion in my face, still wet with tears, and she spoke of my confusion in the following verses:

Muses (handwritten marginal note)

II

He drowns in the depths, his keen mind
dulled in dark brine, far from shore
and, battered by waves the winds whip,
he thrashes in his despair, this man
who once walked the paths of heaven
on solid ground under open skies.
He used to gaze at the sun and study
the constellations of the cold new moon,
and he knew how the evening star of the west
appears in the east to announce the morning
and turns through its steady, stately cycles.
He studied the hidden causes of things
and understood why the winds blow
and lash the waves of the sea. He learned
how fixed stars dance in their figures
and the sun's rising and setting. He studied
how the warmth of the spring calls forth
flowers that bedeck the earth
and how the autumn yields its riches,
the gifts of the fields and fruits of the vine.
He who has seen into Nature's secrets
now lies prostrate, his mind bowed down
by heavy chains that hang from his neck.
With eyes cast down thus, he can see
nothing but dull, brown earth before him.

"But this is the time for treatment," she said, "and not mere complaining." She looked at me with a steady gaze and asked, "Are you the same person who was nourished with my rich milk and fed on my diet as you were growing up? Did I not prepare you with such weapons as you could now use in your difficulties if you had not chosen to discard them? Do you even recognize me? Answer me! Are you silent because you are ashamed? Or are you just dumbstruck? I'd rather that it was shame, but I am afraid that you are merely and deplorably stupefied."

And at this point, seeing that I was speechless, she laid her hand on my chest and said, "He is in no real danger. He merely suffers from a lethargy, a sickness that is common among the depressed. He has forgotten who he really is, but he will recover, for he used to know me, and all I have to do is clear the mist that beclouds his vision."

Then, in a gesture of gentle efficiency, she gathered the skirt of her dress so that with its fabric she could dry the tears from my eyes.

III

The darkness then began to lift as the night frayed,
    or perhaps my eyes cleared and recovered their
        powers.

We have beheld the menacing northwest winds
    pile up
masses of rain clouds that blacken the skies
and hide the light of the sun. The stars have not
    yet appeared,
    but daylight is utterly gone. And then a fresh
north wind from Aeolus' cave comes sweeping
    down to clear
    the illusion of night and restore the shining
        sun
to its proper place in the sky in a glorious
    afternoon
    that invigorates and dazzles our grateful eyes.

It was exactly like that sudden dispersal of clouds
on a dark day with the rays of the sun pouring down
again. I recovered myself enough to recognize now
the face of my healer. As I gazed, her features came
into clear focus and I beheld the nurse who had
reared me and whose house I had visited from my
earliest youth, none other than the lady Philosophy.
I asked her why she had deigned to descend from
her dwelling place in the lofty heavens to this dun-
geon to which I had been banished. Was it to suffer
with me and to share the terrible experience of being falsely accused?

"My poor boy," she replied, "why should I desert
you now? Should I not help you with that burden

Love of
φ is what
got him im-
prisoned

you bear in no small measure because of my teachings and the hatred of my name? Do you suppose I
would be frightened by unmerited accusations? Will
Philosophy abandon an innocent man and not be
a companion to him on his journey? Should I be
distressed by false accusations? I am horrified at such
a thought! I am accustomed to being attacked and
was a veteran of such battles even before the time of
my servant Plato. I have been doing battle forever
against proud stupidity. In Plato's own time, was I
not with his teacher, Socrates, who was put to death
unjustly—a death that turned out in the end to be a
martyr's triumph? After that, the squabbling mobs
of Stoics and Epicureans fought to claim his legacy
and each side tried to carry me off, tearing this lovely
dress I had woven with my own hands so that each
of them could claim to be wearing at least shreds of
my raiment, which they pretended quite absurdly to
be the entire garment. And these bits and patches
were enough for them to gain a certain acceptance
by some and even for them to be attacked sometimes
by the ignorant mob. But even if you had never heard
of Anaxagoras' banishment from Athens, or Socrates
drinking the hemlock, or the torture of Zeno, all
of which happened abroad, surely you would know
about such Romans as Canius, and Seneca, and
Soranus, whose stories are neither so old nor from so
far away. And the only cause of their deaths was their

dedication to me and their indifference to and contempt for the beliefs and pursuits of wicked men that my teaching had instilled in them. It is hardly a surprise, then, that we should be beset by the iniquitous whom it is our purpose in life to displease and confound. And even though there are many of them, we can still despise them because they have no principles to lead them and are motivated only by ignorance and whim that lead them now one way and now another. Sometimes, they come against us in great strength, but Wisdom, our general, withdraws her forces into our stronghold while our enemies wear themselves out plundering our useless baggage trains. From our ramparts we look down and laugh at them as they busy themselves carrying away their pointless, cumbersome trophies. We are protected, after all, by the strength of our citadel from stupidity's disorganized forays."

IV

Who has composed himself in the face of fate
and crushed it beneath his heel? Who has a life
in proper order, prepared for good fortune or
    bad?
Only he can hold his head high,
untroubled by the tides of contingency,

the waves of the sea, Vesuvius' showers of fire,
or the mighty thunderbolts that descend from
    above
to demolish lofty towers. Wretched men
cringe before tyrants who have no power,
the victims of their trivial hopes and fears.
They do not understand that anger is helpless,
fear is pointless, and desire is all a delusion.
He whose heart is fickle is not his own
master, has thrown away his shield, deserted
his post, and he forges the links of the chain that
    holds him.

"Now," she said, "have you understood what I have been saying? Has it sunk in, or are you a donkey hearing a lute? Why are you still weeping? As Homer tells us, 'Speak out, don't hold it, buried in your heart.'* If you want the physician's cure, you must bare your wound."

I summoned my strength somehow and managed to answer, "Look around! Do you need to ask such questions? Is my terrible treatment at Fortune's hands not clear? Look at this dreadful cell! Does it resemble that cozy library where you used to visit in my house, where we would sit and discuss all kinds

* Homer *Iliad* 1.363.

of interesting matters, both human and divine? Was
this what I looked like? Was this the expression on
my face when you showed me the paths of the stars
and how the order of the universe implied an ethical
system for mankind? And is this the reward you had
for me, telling me that I should accept Plato's opinion that governments would be well run if there
were philosopher-kings? You inferred from his writing that philosophers should take part in politics in
order to prevent the state from falling into the hands
of the stupid and the wicked, who would bring ruin
not only to themselves but to good people along with
them. And I listened to you and went into public
life, figuring that I could apply in the real world
those ideas we had been discussing there in the library. God knows—as you do, too—that that was all
I had in mind, to apply myself to the betterment of
the government. And what happened? I found myself inevitably opposing the plans of selfish and un-
principled men, and in the effort to keep my conscience clear and do what was lawful and right, I
offended a lot of people who were more powerful
than I was.

"Whenever Conigastus was trying to swindle
some poor, defenseless fellow, there I would be, in
his way, an increasingly intolerable annoyance to
him. How many times did I speak out against Trig-

[margin note: Questioned b/c of his own arrest/punishment]

guilla, the Palace Prefect, either before he had committed some outrageous violation of law or after the fact? Who was the voice of the victims whenever the rapacious barbarians brought their trumped-up charges against them? And every time I did this, I knew what the dangers were, and I did the right thing anyway, despite the threats of the wicked or their offers of bribes. I was never tempted or intimidated. And when the great provincial families were ruined by avaricious individuals and corrupt officials who together were robbing them blind, I felt their distress as much as any of the victims and raised my voice to protest their sufferings. When the famine hit us and there was a decree ordering the forced sale of foodstuffs that would have ruined the entire province of Campania, I was the one who opposed the Praetorian Prefect and went to the king to protest the enforcement of these outrageous measures, and I won! The dogs of the court were already squabbling about how to divide up the wealth of Paulinus, the ex-consul, when I snatched it back from their slavering jaws. They had already condemned Albinus, another ex-consul, even though he had not yet been tried, and I was the one who interceded, and of course I earned for myself the enmity of Cyprian, the official referee. I was proud of the resentment of these people, and supposed that the fact that I was obligated to nobody would help keep me safe. But there was no one to come to my defense. And who were my accusers? Basil, who had been dismissed from the king's service, was one of them, a man deep in debt who was looking for relief from his obligations. And there were Opilio and Gaudentius, both of them inveterate liars who had been exiled by the king but then asked for sanctuary in some temple. The king found out about this and decreed that unless they left Ravenna by a date certain, he would have them branded on the forehead and then driven out. Can you imagine anything worse than that? And theirs were the names on the accusation against me. How could any sensible person looking at who I was and who they were have trouble deciding whom to believe? You would think that Fortune herself would blush in shame for innocence to be accused by such villains as these!

"And do you know what the charge was against me? That I wanted to protect the Senate! The accusation was that I had prevented those accusers from bringing forth charges that might have convicted the Senate of treason. Can you believe that? And what am I supposed to do, deny the charge, so that you won't be ashamed of me? But I can't deny it because I did want to protect the Senate and the senatorial order, and I can't see how I could ever be persuaded that I was wrong. But the deadline has passed for me to reply to the charges and accuse my accusers. And anyway, since the accusation has been filed against me, defense of the Senate has become a crime. Not that such legalistic games have anything to do with right and wrong. They are fooling themselves to suppose that they can get away with such maneuvers. I am with Socrates in this, that it is wrong for me to assent to a lie or to obscure the truth—and I leave it to you to judge what the truth is in this sorry business—to you and to all philosophers, now and in generations to come. I have written it all down so that there is a record, even though it was extremely distasteful to have to discuss these absurd forgeries in which I am accused of having tried to protect Roman liberties.

"Every now and then, I lay down my quill and ask myself what is the point of this exercise. These forgeries and lies accuse me of protecting Roman freedom. Do I have to try to exonerate myself from such a charge? Is my innocence not immediately apparent, from the absurdity of the charges themselves? I have not been allowed to examine the prosecution's documents, to which the system gives enormous weight. But even if I had been given access to everything, what would there be to say that would be different from Canius' reply to Caligula, when that emperor accused him of knowledge of a conspiracy against his person? 'Had I known of it,' Canius answered, 'you would not.'

"In this sad business, I am not so much overwhelmed by my grief as I am amazed by the idea of wicked men attempting to do evil to virtue. And I am surprised that they have so well succeeded in their efforts. Many people have evil ideas and wicked intentions and hatch nefarious schemes, but to carry out one of these plans is, under God's watchful eye, a truly monstrous thing. And it was in such a circumstance as this that one of your disciples asked how, if there is a God, there can be evil. And if there is not a God, where does good come from?

"Let us suppose, purely hypothetically, that these evil men have some cause to complain, some legitimate grudge against the Senate. Why would they want my blood as well, when they saw me fighting for the oppressed and for the institution of the Senate? Surely, I deserved gentler treatment than the senators themselves! You will remember, because you were always at my side, how at Verona King Theodoric tried to expand the charges of treason that had been lodged against Albinus to include the entire senatorial order. I defended them, without giving a thought to any danger to which I might be subjecting myself. You know that this is, first of all, the truth, and also that I dislike boasting and self-congratulation. The secret pleasure of doing the right thing is vitiated if a man brags about it. But you see the point I'm driving at—that instead of being rewarded for my actual virtue, I am punished for imaginary crimes. And no confession of a crime, however serious, ever found a jury so unanimous in the severity of their judgment, mollified neither by their understanding of general human weakness nor by the impossibility ever of knowing the entire truth. If I had been charged with planning to burn down churches and murder priests or to massacre all men of wealth and title, I would still have had a right either to confess to it or to be hauled into a court for a hearing and there found guilty. But here I am, almost five hundred miles from home, condemned to death and all my property confiscated for having defended the Senate. And without any right to speak in my own defense! Whatever I may have done, I did not deserve to be treated in this way for a charge such as this.

"My accusers know that this is all nonsense, and they dress up their accusations with the further slander that I committed some kind of sacrilege in campaigning for high office. But you, Lady, were with me every moment of the day and night and drove from my mind any thought whatever of ambition or profit.

You instilled into my marrow the Pythagorean motto, *epou theo* (follow God). Now, if you were trying to set my feet upon such a path, would I ever be tempted to listen to the lesser angels that might tempt me? Besides, my house has no secrets and my reputation with my friends who are men of honor and with Symmachus, my father-in-law—who is to be respected almost as much as you are yourself—is such that one would think me above any suspicion of such wickedness. They are the wicked ones, the impious ones, the 'usual suspects,' as it were, and they are so lacking in principle that they implicate you as well in this terrible charge. That I am trained in your disciplines and influenced by your wisdom is offensive to them and seems to them somehow to prove that I have been engaged in wrongdoing. It isn't just that my devotion to you has not been helpful to me, but that they have made you a victim of the hatred that ought properly to have me alone as its target. The world judges actions not on their merit but on their results, which are often a matter of pure chance. Men admire nothing more than success, however achieved. And among the burdens that weigh on me is this idea that, if actions are judged only by outcomes, then those who are, like me, unfortunate or unlucky are likely to be immediately abandoned by men of goodwill. Anyone charged with a crime is

And hatred of one should be aimed @ Socrate

presumed to be guilty, and wild rumors circulate about me and my case as they always do about any poor unfortunate who is charged with any crime. I am thus stripped of my honors, deprived of all my possessions, the subject of wicked gossip, and punished for all my years of faithful and honest service, while the wicked, dancing in their delight, plot new accusations and hatch new schemes. Good men, finding themselves without protection or even the chance to defend themselves, quake in fear as they contemplate what has happened to me, while the bad are emboldened to further offenses.

"It is a sad business, and I am prompted to sing:"

V

Starmaker, master of spheres,
at whose command the heavens spin
in the constellations' dance that you
on your steady throne have choreographed,
bright stars grow dim as you bring on the moon,
crescent or gibbous, reflecting her brother's
dazzling fire, but then she grows pale
herself as he draws near in splendor.
In the evening, Venus rises bright
but loses luster in morning's sunrise,
playing the role that you have assigned her.

When leaves fall and the cold of winter
blows from the north, our days diminish,
but then, in summer's burgeoning heat
the dark hours of nighttime dwindle
as the year fulfills its obligations.
Not even the blowing winds are random,
but Boreas strips leaves from the trees
and Zephyrus brings on gentling nurture.
The Dog Star watches as heat beats down
on crops in the fields, as you, too, observe
and order all from your high office
in your certain purpose, according to plan.
Only man is endowed with freedom
that you could constrain but have chosen not to,
and slippery Fortune plays her random
games with us. The innocent suffer
penalties proper to malefactors
and wicked men sit upon thrones.
Villains thrive and trample the necks
of virtuous men into the mud
of calumny and innuendo,
where the glow of goodness cannot be glimpsed.
They swear falsely and deck themselves
in duplicity's gaudy raiment, impressive
to gullible crowds that grant them respect.
They play with their power and topple kings,
and everywhere on the wretched earth
men at their hearthsides huddle in fear.

Look down from on high and impose your
    correction,
you who bind all the world with your laws,
who control the waves and the tides, bring order
to the surging waves of mankind's follies,
and steady us with your hand's firmness,
and whose awesome power we see in the skies.

I had come to the end of my loud lamentation,
but Philosophy appeared to be entirely unmoved.
With a calm, businesslike expression, she looked at
me and said, "As soon as I saw you with your
tearstained face, I knew that you were suffering, and
I understood that you had been banished. Unless
you had mentioned it, I would not have supposed
how far you had been sent away; but this banishment is not merely geographical, is it? You have been
banished from yourself, and one could even say that
you are therefore the instrument of your own torments, for no one else could have done this to you.
You seem to have forgotten what your native country is. It is not a democracy like old Athens, but as
Homer says, 'There is one rule, the one king,'* and
he is a friend to his subjects and never sends them
into exile. To obey his justice is the only freedom.

* Homer *Iliad* 2.204–205.

The basic law of your country is that any man who has chosen to live there cannot be banished from within its strong walls and deep moat. But if anyone no longer wants to live there, then he no longer deserves to do so.

"What most moves me, then, is not the look of this place but your own sorry appearance. I don't need a library with comfortable chairs, ivory gewgaws, and big glass windows, but rather the workroom of your mind, for it isn't the books that are important but the ideas in them, the opinions and principles of times gone by, which is what gives the books their value.

"What you have said about your conduct in public life is quite true, and you have not mentioned anywhere near all the decent and proper things that you have done and tried to do. You have referred to the falsity of the accusations against you, and the world knows that you are correct in this, too. The crimes of your enemies are the talk of the people everywhere, and they tell each other the sorry and sordid details that you have not bothered to recite to me. You spoke of the Senate's unjust behavior and expressed your regret that I have been included in these calumnies, and you have wept about the damage to my reputation. And you have shown your anger at the workings of Fortune and how rewards and punishments seem to have little to do with what people deserve. Indeed, your poem invokes the order of the universe and asks that heaven intercede here on earth.

"But to tell you the truth, you are confused. You are torn by grief and anger and self-pity, and each of these pulls you in a different direction. You are not yet ready for strong medicines, I'm afraid, so we shall begin with something milder, anodynes, so that the sore and angry places may be softened and soothed. Then we can perhaps begin the real treatment of your complaints."

VI

In the house of Cancer, the sun beats down
on furrows too hot and dry to receive
the seeds farmers might think to sow,
and, hungry, they must wander the woods
looking for bitter acorns to eat.
No one would think to gather violets
when north winds bring the cold of winter,
or attempt to prune his grapevines in spring.
Autumn is Bacchus' proper season,
for God has marked out the year's order,
and does not allow for change or appeal.

Whoever defies the laws of nature
must come to ruin and rue his folly.

"Let us begin, then," she said, "with a few simple
questions that will help in the diagnosis."

"Ask away," I told her. "I will answer."

"Is it your view that life is a series of chance events?
Or do you think it has an order and a rationale?"

"If you look at the natural world," I said, "there
appears to be an order. I believe that there is a God
and that he watches over his creation. I can't imagine a time when I could abandon such a belief."

"That was what your poem was about, I believe—
that there is an order in nature but not, apparently,
in the affairs of men, which alone seem to be outside
God's control. But your healthy belief in the order of
nature does not seem to enable you to resist your
sickness, so let us explore a little more deeply. There
is some connection that is apparently missing. You
say that you believe in a God that governs the world,
but how do you suppose he does this? By what means
does he guide natural events?"

"I can't answer that. I don't even understand the
question."

"Ah, then there is something missing, isn't there?
Your defenses have been breached and there is a gap
in your fortifications through which the fever of

emotion has managed to insinuate itself. Tell me this. Do you remember the purpose of things and the goal of Nature's order?"

"I used to know that, but in my grief, I can't remember."

"Well, what is the source of all things?"

"God," I said, albeit tentatively.

"But how can you remember the beginning of things and not remember their end? You are distracted, it would appear, but not totally undone. Tell me this. Do you remember that you are a man?"

"Yes, of course."

"And what is a man?" she asked.

"Are you asking me if I believe that man is a mortal, rational animal? Both of those things are certainly true."

"But are you not something more?"

"I don't think so, no."

After a brief pause, she said, "I see. And I understand the cause of your sickness. You have forgotten what you are. I see why and how you are ill, and I also see the way to cure you. It is what you cannot remember that causes you to feel lost and to grieve about your exile and the loss of your property. If you cannot remember the goal of all things, then you suppose that wicked men have power and luck. And because you have forgotten how the world is ordered, you imagine that there is nothing but the vicissitudes of Fortune. This is enough not only to cause serious illness but even death. But the author of all health has not yet abandoned you and you have not totally lost your true nature. The best cure there is for such a disease as the one afflicting you is a correct understanding of the governance of the world, which is not merely a string of random events but the result of divine reason.

"Take heart," she said, "for there is still a spark of life in you that we can rekindle and restore so that it is a healthy fire. But we are not yet at the moment when we can resort to the strongest medicines. The way men's minds work is that when they lose sight of some correct opinion, a false one comes to take its place, and confusion arises, a kind of fog that obscures clear vision. I shall try to clear some of that fog for you, and then you may be able to see your way to the shining light of the truth that never dims."

VII

The darkness of clouds
hides the stars.
The clear-glass sea
whipped by the wind

becomes opaque,
a wall of waves
with the mud stirred up
that blackens it further.
A crystal brook
encountering rocks
from the heights above
can be stopped in its bed.
Your mind is likewise
clouded and blocked.
But the right road
awaits you still.
Cast out your doubts,
your fears and desires,
let go of grief
and of hope as well,
for where these rule
the mind is their subject.

❧❧BOOK II❧❧

I

She was silent for quite a while, which was perhaps a show of modesty but in fact served to focus my attention so that I was waiting with particular concentration for what she might say next. And then she spoke: "If I understand you and your sickness properly, the situation is one in which you are longing for your previous good fortune. It is this change in fortune that you are convinced has affected your spirit, bringing on this depression from which you suffer. Fortune, of course, is a monster, and she toys with those for whom she intends catastrophe, showing her friendly face and lifting them up before dashing them down when they are least prepared for it. Think about that. You know what she is like and how she behaves, and you know, too, that anything you had from her hands was not worth having, and in losing those things you have lost nothing of importance. It should not be difficult for me to persuade you of the truth of what I am saying. You will recog-

nize it at once, I think, and you will recall that when you were basking in her smiles, you spoke often about her treacheries and produced arguments from our own sanctum that you delivered in the strongest possible language.

"Even so, a tumble of the kind you have taken, a complete reversal of your affairs, is not pleasant and is likely to produce some temporary disturbance in the mind. And it is time, I think, for you to take some mild palliative that will, when you have absorbed it, prepare you for those stronger preparations that will be curative. Let us begin with the pleasant devices of rhetoric that are reliable only if they do not stray from our fundamental principles. We must be careful that it harmonizes properly with the modes of our preferred music.

"Now, what is it that is actually upsetting you and has driven you to such fits of weeping? You have had a sharp bump, and you think that Fortune's attitude toward you has changed. But you're wrong. She hasn't changed a bit. She was always whimsical, and she remains constant to her inconstancy. You were wrong to take her smiles seriously and to rely on them as the basis for your happiness. Now, what you have learned is that the changing face of blind power is unreliable—and always was. Other men may not understand this, but she has revealed herself entirely to you. If you want to be one of her followers, then follow, but without complaint. If you spurn her treachery, then reject her absolutely as one who plays such games with men's lives. You blame her for your sorrows, but your heart ought to be at rest, for, now that she has left you, you know not to trust her. And no one will ever feel sure that she is not going to abandon him just as she abandoned you.

"Or is it that lost happiness that you mourn? Was that good fortune so dear to you, even though you should have understood that it couldn't be trusted and was, therefore, never really yours? It doesn't stay, it doesn't last, and when it leaves, you are bereft? You should have recognized that it was never in your control and that the visit of the unreliable goddess is a sure sign of misery to come. You should never confine your attention to what is before your eyes at the moment but consider too what the future is likely to bring. You knew the mutability of Fortune and you should have inured yourself against her constant threats of betrayal that too often inspire fear and flattery from those she has momentarily graced. If you submit your neck to her yoke, you cannot then complain about what happens to you or how the mistress you have yourself chosen is treating you badly. You can no longer bargain with her, tell her what is fair, or how long she should stay, or under what circumstances she may depart from you. If you spread your sails before the wind, then you must go where the wind takes you and not where you might wish to go. You want to try farming and sow your seeds in the earth, then you must expect barren years as well as years of abundance. If you worship her, then you are her slave and cannot question her. Would you presume to stop that wheel of hers from turning? If you could do that, it would no longer be the wheel of Fortune, would it?"

With an indifferent hand she spins the wheel,
     and one or another
number comes up lucky, while the only constant
     is change,
the ebb and flow of a tide like that of Euripus'
     strait.
Mighty kings are brought low and the weeping
     face of the conquered
is lifted, but for only a moment, as if to mock him.
To the cries and complaints of men she pays no
     mind whatever,
and she even laughs at their piteous groans that
     she has evinced.
It's a game she plays and a demonstration of
     ruthless power,
a way to keep her devotees in a total subjection,

raising men up and then dashing them down in
ruin.

II

"But let me take Fortune's part, argue her case, and
then ask you whether you have any just complaint
against her. What she would certainly say would be:
'What complaint have you to make against me?
What harm have I done to you? What possessions of
yours have I taken? For that matter, can any mortal
actually claim ownership of any possession or office
or claim title to these things before any judge in the
world? If you can find anyone who takes such a view,
I shall return everything to you that was legitimately
yours. But when nature brought you out of your
mother's womb, you were naked and poor, and helpless. And I accepted you and was kind to you. I pam-
pered you and gave you more than you needed. Indeed, one could say that I spoiled you and that is why
you are now so angry with me. I gave you all kinds of
affluence and luxury, whatever was in my power, and
you took it as if it were your right. Now that I have
taken it back, you ought to thank me for the use of
what was always mine anyway rather than complain
of the loss of what was never yours. Why complain

or protest? I have done you no harm but have only withdrawn the wealth and honors that everyone knew were mine to bestow. I have recalled my servants from you, and they have been obedient and have returned to me. I am their mistress, after all. If those things you complain about losing were really yours, you'd still have them. But they were mine, and I had the owner's rights to them, which I chose to exercise. The sky is bright and clear sometimes, and then, on other days, it is dark and cloudy. The year has seasons of warmth and growth with fruits and flowers, and then it has times of cold and rain. The sea is smooth and pleasant on occasion, but then it can be stormy with great waves and winds. Am I the only one who must defer to men's desires that I be consistent in a way that is quite foreign to my nature? That my nature is changeable you know perfectly well. I have a wheel, and I turn it so that what is low is raised high and what is up is brought down. You ascend? Fine! But you must acknowledge that it can't be wrong for you to have to descend again. You were not unaware of how a wheel works.

"Do you not know the story of Croesus, the king of Lydia who was once such a menace to the great Cyrus but then was condemned to be burnt alive and was only saved by a sudden rainstorm? Have you forgotten how the good Aemilius Paulus shed tears over the fate of his captive, King Peres of Macedonia? What else is tragedy but the sad story of happy men who are overthrown by the blows of fortune? Did you not learn as a young man that Jupiter has on his threshold "two jars, with evils in one and blessings in the other"?* You have had more than an average share of the good things I can give, but even now I have not deserted you entirely, for my mutability still gives you reason to hope for better things to come. But it is irrational to pine away and to suppose that you are different from the rest of mankind and that you live under a law that applies only to yourself.'"

Wow, sneaky!

> Should Plenty ever pour out riches
>   abundant as sands on a beach
> that the waves pile up, or the stars in the clear
>   night sky, without stinting,
> men would not cease their endless complaining
>   and pleading always for more.
> If God were prodigal, showering gold
>   in answer to every prayer,
> and heaping honors on every head,
>   they would not be content,
> never mind grateful. They'd take it for granted.
>   Greed opens new maws.

Bruce Almighty!

---

* Homer *Iliad* 24.527.

There are no limits, no satiation,
    even in those who choke
on their wealth and good fortune. Their thirsts
      yet
      burn with poverty's need.

III

"Now, supposing that Fortune spoke to you in such a way. What could your answer possibly be? If you have anything to justify your complaints that I haven't thought of, then, by all means, tell me what it is! Explain it to me."

"What you have said," I answered, "is all rhetoric. It is a plausible series of high-sounding phrases. A man can listen to them and even be beguiled, but his sense of having been injured lies much deeper than that. He listens to the arguments and follows along, but the moment they stop, he is again reminded of the grief that gnaws at his heart."

"That's quite true," she said. "But, as you remember, this was not supposed to be a cure, but only a kind of dressing for your wound, which is very tender. When the right time comes, there will be stronger medicines. But it is also true that there is no particular reason for you to want pity. Have you already forgotten the number and extent of the blessings that you used to enjoy? When your father died, you were cared for by men of the very highest rank, and you married into the families that were the most distinguished of the nation's citizens. And even before you joined their families, you had won their love and friendship, which is perhaps even more valuable. All the world called you the happiest of men, married into such a family, with a chaste and loving wife and with the blessing of two fine sons. It would be tedious to list the honors that were bestowed upon you in your youth that older men envied. Let us skip on to the pinnacle of your achievement, which was your greatest distinction. And I ask you, if any happiness can come from success in the affairs of men, then how could the weight of your present misfortunes obliterate the memory of that spectacular day when you saw your two sons carried from your house to ascend to their joint consulship? That was the day they took their seats in the curule chairs in the senate to hear you deliver your oration in honor of the king! And later that day, you were between them in the stadium with the mob crowding around you as if it were a military triumph!

"You had nothing but praise then for the works of Fortune, when she was coddling you as her pet. You had gifts from her as are rarely given to a private citizen. And now you want to reckon up your accounts with her? This is the first time she has shown you anything other than a beatific smile! Balance out the good things and the bad that have happened in your life and you will have to acknowledge that you are still way ahead. You are unhappy because you have lost those things in which you took pleasure? But you can also take comfort in the likelihood that what is now making you miserable will also pass away. You enter this situation in life for the first time, a new-comer and a stranger. But a part of you always knew that there is no constancy in human affairs, and that time brings change inevitably. Even a man who never has the kind of catastrophe that befell you comes to the last days of his life when he sees that his good fortune is finally ending. And do you suppose it makes any difference to him at such a moment whether good fortune is leaving him or he is leaving good fortune?"

When Phoebus from his chariot spreads
    light through the looming sky,
his bright flame overwhelms the twinkle of stars.
    When Zephyr's gentle breath
warms the springtime, roses bud.
    But a sudden storm from the south

can strip the bushes to bare thorns.
The sea, sometimes serene,
glints a pale and unruffled blue,
but the north wind assails it,
and the storms rage and the sea churns.
The beauty of earth changes.
Enjoy it but never think to trust it.
As with the fleeting pleasures
of men, a stern law decrees
that nothing in life lasts.

IV

I answered, "Yes, what you say is true enough. You, who are the nurse of all the virtues, know that I did enjoy, if briefly, a great prosperity. But it is also true that the worst kind of misfortune is one that befalls someone who has previously known happiness."

"No," she said patiently. "You are suffering because of your incorrect beliefs. If you put all that emphasis on the vacuous idea of fortuitous happiness, then you would have to admit to me that you are still relatively well off. If, by God's will, one of your most precious possessions is preserved unharmed, can you talk about your misfortune as being utter and absolute? Your most esteemed father-in-law, Symmachus, a man entirely wise and virtuous, is safe. And you would be willing in a minute to purchase such wisdom and goodness at the cost of your life. But he is lamenting your troubles, without any concern for his own difficulties. Your wife, that excellent woman, is alive, although for your sake she is most unhappy. And I grant you that her unhappiness is a legitimate cause of your distress, that she is spending her days weeping and longing for you. And I do not need to burden you with any reference to your two sons, who are both consuls, and who display such a commendable likeness to their father and their grandfather. Now, I realize that men are concerned with preserving their own lives, but it ought to be of some help that you can recognize those blessings you still possess, which everyone would agree are dearer than life itself. So stop your weeping. Fortune does not hate everyone in your family, and when those anchors still hold fast, the storm, however violent, is not overwhelming. You have present consolation and you have hope for the future."

"I pray that those anchors may continue to hold," I said. "And you are right. As long as I have them, I shall probably not drown. But you can nevertheless understand how my life has deteriorated from my recent prosperity."

She nodded and said, "But we are making progress, one small step at a time. You are no longer bewailing everything but have begun to focus, which is a good thing. It is difficult for both of us if you wallow in grief and universalize it, complaining that if you are not absolutely happy then you must be absolutely miserable. After all, who is so happy that there is not a single thing he wouldn't prefer to change? The human condition is such that even the most fortunate are not free from worry. Good fortune is not something we possess entirely or forever. One man owns a lot of property and is prosperous enough, but he is ashamed of his undistinguished forebears. Another is of high birth but never goes anywhere because he is ashamed of how poor he is. A third is both well born and rich enough, but he is unmarried. And a fourth, happily married, is miserable because he has not been blessed with children, and he knows that his estate will therefore pass on to someone else's children. And then a fifth, who has children, is unhappy because his sons or daughters have not turned out well and have disappointed him. There is hardly anyone anywhere who is without something to fret about. And, almost always, people on the outside have no hint whatever of what is troubling the hearts and souls of their friends or associates. Consider, too, that most people who are ex-

tremely lucky in their lives are the most sensitive to
any slight adversity, because they aren't used to having to deal with disappointments and frustrations,
and therefore they are the most easily upset. There
are people in the world who would trade places with
you—just as you are now—and think that they were
in heaven. This place that you complain about as remote and an exile is home to the people who live
here. Almost nothing is inherently miserable, unless
you think it is. And contrariwise, a man who knows
how to find contentment can be happy in almost any
circumstance. Whose happiness is so complete that,
if he were in a mood to complain, he could not find
something he might prefer to change or improve?
And how is it that troubles, however bitter, can be-
smirch a man's contented mood? Happiness is a
good thing, surely, but it is a mood and no matter
how pleasant it may be, one cannot prevent its passing when it will, as moods do. Which means that
happiness itself is wretched, inasmuch as it neither
endures reliably nor, even when it is present, satis-
fies.

"Why then do men look outside themselves for
happiness when it is surely to be found inside? It is
error that confuses you, and ignorance. Let us explore this just a little. Is there anything more precious to you than yourself? No, certainly not. But if

you are in possession of yourself, then you have that which you don't want to lose and which Fortune cannot take away from you. To understand how happiness cannot depend on fortuitous external circumstances, think about the question this way. If happiness is the highest good of a rational man, and if whatever can be taken away cannot be the highest good (because that which can't be taken away must be a higher good), then it makes no sense to say that good fortune can supply happiness. Or look at it another way and ask of a man who has been having a run of good luck whether he knows or doesn't know that it can be taken away. If he doesn't know, then he can't be happy but only ignorant; and if he does know, then he can't be happy because he is worried about losing everything at any moment, and this continual fear will keep him from being happy. Or there is a third possibility, which is that he thinks it won't matter when he loses it all. But in that case, he doesn't value it very much and doesn't care about what he can so calmly imagine losing.

"Now, you used to like this kind of reasoned discussion, and I remember that you used to maintain that the minds of men are immortal while assuredly the bodies of men are subject to happenstance and in any event are mortal and will die. If you still hold that position, it is difficult to see how you would argue that bodily pleasure can bring happiness, if every kind of mortal thing is fated to descend into misery and death. On the other hand, we know that many men have looked for happiness through death and even through pain and suffering. How, then, can this present life make them happy when the prospect of its end does not make them miserable?"

He who would build a sturdy
    house he intends will last,
that will not be destroyed
    by the force of the winds and waves,
would do well to select his site
    with a certain degree of prudence,
avoiding the mountaintops
    where the gales buffet and rage
and the desert dunes where the sands
    will erode beneath his foundation.
Those places are pretty enough,
    but danger is part of their nature,
and no one ought to be reckless.
    Build upon low rock,
where you're safe from the gales and the thunder,
    and far from the turbulent sea,
where no one is ever secure.
    Within the strength of your walls

you have some hope of survival
and may smile at the hostile skies.

[handwritten annotation: → Beauty! Sounds like a song title]

V

"Now that your initial tenderness has been some-what relieved, we can perhaps go on to some stronger remedies. Let us suppose for the moment that the gifts of Fortune were not all temporary; still, is there anything among them that would not, on close scrutiny, turn out to be worthless? Are riches ever really yours? Are they valuable in themselves? And where would that value be? In the piles of gold? The financial statements? It seems to me that wealth is more splendid in the spending of it than in the getting of it. Avarice is not admirable, but liberality is generally praised. So money is precious not when you have it but when it passes on from you to somebody else, in which case you don't have it anymore. Imagine if you will that a single man had all the money in the world. The rest of mankind would have to manage to live without it. The voice of one orator fills all the ears in the audience at once, but your wealth cannot pass on to many unless it is divided up into tiny allotments. And the giver becomes necessarily poorer! So what is so wonderful about money? It cannot be shared with many men, and it cannot be possessed without making others poorer.

"Are you dazzled, perhaps, by the glitter of jewels? Even if you are, you must admit that the sparkle is that of the gems themselves and has nothing to do with the men who may admire them. What is it about them that a rational man could find to admire? There is no movement of living spirit that a rational person could think of as beautiful. They are the work of the Creator, and there is a kind of attractiveness of a lower order, but they come nowhere near the excellence of a man, do they? They can't be worth a man's admiration!

"Or perhaps it is the beauty of the countryside that you find pleasing. And why not, after all? It is a part of the creation, which is, indeed, beautiful. In the same way, we can take pleasure in a view of the sea when it is calm, and we can admire the sky with the myriad stars and the moon and, in the daytime, the sun. But do any of these things in any way belong to you? Can you claim for yourself any part of their splendor? Are they your flowers that bloom in the spring? Are they your fruits that grow on the trees in the summertime? Why are you so fascinated by these things and why do you embrace them as if they were your own? Fortune will never give you what nature has intended otherwise. The fruits of the earth are meant for the nourishment of living things, and, by all means, take what you need. But there is no point in asking Fortune for more than that. It is absurd to go from contentment to superfluity, because what you add will be either unpleasant or actually harmful.

"Is it clothing that you enjoy? But if you look good, I either admire the skill of the tailor or the quality of the material. Servants then? But they are a great burden in a household, and often dishonest and even dangerous. But even if they happen to be honest, how is that virtue of theirs attributed to you or counted as a part of what you possess? So all those things that you enjoy turn out to have nothing to do with you. None of those goods is yours. And if they have no value or beauty that you could have claimed, why would you mourn their loss? They were precious only because you thought of them as precious and enjoyed adding them up as if they were your belongings.

"But what is it that you really want? You want to fortify yourself against need by storing up plenty, and yet what you do has exactly the opposite effect. You have precious furniture, but that requires guards. Those who have a lot need a lot. It's expensive to be rich! Those who have almost nothing measure themselves by the requirements of nature rather than by the extravagances of ambition or vanity. Are you not able to find value in yourself? If you could see that, you wouldn't need all those external trinkets. Is your world so topsy-turvy that a living, rational, almost godlike being would need the possession of all this lifeless stuff to be happy? Other creatures are content being what they are. But men, who are rational and godlike, need to bedeck themselves with finery in order to be happy, and you don't seem to understand that this is actually insulting to your maker. He appointed men to be the lords of earth and you contrive to reduce yourselves to a base dependency. If a good thing is of greater worth than the person it belongs to, then, when you put all this value on things, you reduce yourself in your own estimation and become, yourself, all but valueless. Man is better than other things—but only if he knows who and what he is! If he forgets himself, then he is lower than the beasts. Animals don't have self-knowledge or self-awareness. And in man it can prove to be a fault, for you can wander from right reason when you imagine that you can improve yourself by putting on the beauties of other things. It's ridiculous! You have a package with fine wrappings, but what is underneath is foul and worthless.

"My view is that nothing is good that is harmful to him who owns it. Do you disagree? Of course not! But riches have very often harmed those who possess them, because every man turns envious and greedy and supposes that he has a better right to the loot and wants all the gold and jewels for himself. So there you are, with your stuff, and you find yourself fearful about being waylaid or even murdered for your possessions. Meanwhile, if you had set out on your journey with nothing at all, you wouldn't be troubled by the thought of robbers. So what good are riches if they cost you your sense of security and *Irony* safety?"

How happy were men long ago,
when they were content with nature
and not yet corrupted by wealth:
their hungers were easily sated
by acorns they found on the ground.
They had not yet learned to mix
sweet honey into their wine.
They did not dress up in silks
dyed bright with Tyrian purple.
They fell asleep on the grass
and drank from a nearby stream.
In the hot noons they would sit

in the shade of a towering pine.
They did not chop down these trees
to fashion the keels of boats
to sail on the seas and venture
to unknown shores and peoples.
No bugle calls then had sounded
to summon men to bloodshed
in hatred or naked greed
that stained the fields with blood,
for what could men gain from killing?
Look at us now and compare
our lives to those of the ancients.
As fierce as the fires of Etna
is the lust of men for plunder.
Shame, shame on the man
who first dug gold from the earth
and brought the bright baubles of jewelers
into the light of the sun.

VI

"And what shall I say about those high offices you
held and all that power you had? You mourn their
loss too and talk about how wonderful they were,
but without any real understanding of their true
worth. After all, when power like that falls into the

hands of the wrong men, it can be as harmful as the eruptions of Etna or the worst of floods. You are aware, I am sure, of how the old Romans wanted to abolish the power of the consuls that once had been the bastions of Roman liberty but had turned into something quite different as the consuls became proud and arrogant. It was the same kind of arrogance that had caused the Romans to seize power from their kings and even to change the name of the ruler's office! I grant you that there are times—not many, I'm afraid—when power has been given to good men, but in those circumstances, the only good in the power has come from the goodness of the men who possessed it. It is not that a man of virtue is honored because of high office, but rather that the office is honored because of his virtue.

"And what did that great power of yours amount to, after all? You are all earthbound animals, are you not? And if you saw a mouse that somehow claimed to have authority over all the other mice . . . would you not laugh? What are men, anyway, when you come right down to it, but relatively weak creatures whom a fly or a mosquito can kill with a bite or a worm can debilitate, insinuating itself inside him. What power does one man exert over another except over his body, or over what is of even less worth than his body, which is to say his fortune? A free mind cannot be commanded. The natural calm of a composed mind that has reason at its disposal cannot be disturbed. When the tyrant Nicocreon thought to use torture to force Anaxarchus, a free man, into betraying his friends, that philosopher bit off his tongue and spat it in the tyrant's face. And by this means, the very torture that the tyrant thought was the instrument of his cruelty became Anaxarchus' weapon of virtue. Busirus used to murder his guests, until one of them, Hercules, murdered him instead. Regulus chained many Carthaginian prisoners of war, and then he found his own hands bound in chains by his captors. As you think about such stories, can you maintain that one man has power over another who can never be certain that such power may not one day be used against him?

"Think, too, how, if those offices and their powers had anything inherently good in them, they would never be possessed by wicked men, for in nature opposites do not attract one another. And since there can be no doubt that offices are often held by evil men, then it follows that they are not in themselves good. And the same thing can be said about all the gifts of Fortune, which so many evil men enjoy so often. Consider the case of a man we call brave—whom we see to be behaving bravely. Or a swift runner is one who demonstrates swiftness. The practice of an art can be a manifestation of talent, as the practice of medicine can show that a man has knowledge and concern and is a doctor. A man who can give a re-sounding and persuasive speech we call eloquent. Each of these qualities is demonstrated in the behavior of the person to whom we attribute them. And each quality necessarily rejects whatever is contrary to it. But riches do not get rid of avarice, nor can power give a man moderation and self-control if power is what he lusts after. High office, then, when it is given to a dishonest man, does not make him worthy of it but rather displays his unworthiness to the world. And what does all this mean? It means, I think, that you give wrong names to things, and if you examine carefully what each thing is in itself, then you find that the label is false. Wealth is not really wealth, and power is not really power, just as honor turns out not really to be honor. And we may extend this to include all of a man's fortune, in which there turns out to be nothing worth seeking. Fortune has nothing whatever to do with goodness, since she does not confine herself to good men nor does she make good those who enjoy her favors."

We know how the heart of man is savage,
when cities are blazing and senators killed,
when brother murders a brother, his hand

dripping still with their mother's gore.
How could Nero look at her cold
corpse with dry eyes and praise its beauty?
But his scepter extended its influence
throughout the world to the westering waves,
to the lands in the east where the sun rises
and the Great Bear looks down with indifference,
and the south with the desert's sweltering sands.
Could all this power restrain his madness,
sharp as a sword and bitter as poison?

VII

I answered her, "You know perfectly well that ambition played a very small part in my choice of career. What I wanted was a chance to take part in the affairs of state so that those virtues I had might be of some benefit to others. It seemed to me a duty to contribute what I could and not let my abilities go to waste."

She pursed her lips slightly and then replied, "That would have a certain appeal to minds that are exceptional and able, but not yet brought to the fulfillment and perfection of their virtues. What you are talking about is still the desire for glory, for recognition for your great services to the state. But you have now begun to learn how insubstantial that fame is. For one thing, you have studied astronomy and you know how tiny the earth is in the vast spaces of the heavens. You know from Ptolemy how little of the universe is inhabited by living things. And if you subtract from Ptolemy's calculations the area on earth that is covered by seas or marshes or deserts, there is only a small space where men can thrive. Now is it in this little niche in the universe that you want to spread your reputation and memorialize your name? What could be the point? And add to what I've said the fact that in our small habitable space, there are many nations, and many languages, and many different customs among peoples we may trade with but whom we don't know at all. How does your ambition seem then? Never mind the fame of individual men; there are entire cities that you have never heard of. Do you remember that Cicero says somewhere that the fame of Rome has not gone beyond the Caucasus, and he said that when Rome was at the height of its power and was feared by the Parthians and other people in that part of the world. Now, even in this little speck in the universe that we live in, do you suppose the fame of a single Roman can go where the glory of Rome itself cannot? And anyway, with the customs of different peoples varying so widely, what is revered in one place may be de-

(margin, handwritten) Desire for glory... But in perspective

spised in another. If you are known abroad, it is all but certain that you will be misunderstood there. Each person, then, must be content to be known within the bounds of his own country.

"Think, also, of how many people, famous in their own time, are altogether forgotten now. Either there was no written record, or, if there was, then the writers are lost or forgotten in the shimmer of time. And do you still think that you can succeed at those odds and that your fame will somehow endure? And for how long? A thousand years? Even that is only a moment in the infinite stretch of the eons. You know that you can't compare the finite with the infinite. And even if your fame were to last that millennium we were speaking of, that would mean nothing—not just small but absolutely nonexistent. And still, there you were, doing the political thing, testing the changing winds of popularity, listening to empty rumors, and ignoring the dictates of your own virtue as you deferred to the prattle of the mob.

"You thought you were a philosopher, but let me tell you a story. There was a man who made such a claim, not from a dedication to truth and reason but out of vanity, as a way of enhancing his reputation. Somebody came along to taunt him and suggested that he was a fraud. And this critic said that he would believe the claim if the man could bear all the inju-

ries fate heaped upon him in calm and in silence.
Then he would admit that the fellow was a philosopher. Well, the other one adopted a patient manner
and for months and even years bore up under the in-
sults and injuries of life. And then he asked his chal-
lenger, 'Now do you admit that I am a philosopher?'
To which the reply was, 'I would have, if you had
kept silent.'

"But let us be serious. What has fame to offer to
virtuous men after death destroys the body? If men
disappear utterly—which we cannot believe—then
glory is nothing at all because he to whom it attaches
will not exist. But if there is a mind that is let loose at
last from its earthly prison and is free to return to its
heavenly home, will it care any longer about mere
earthly affairs? Will it not rather, in its seat on high,
prefer to rejoice in its liberation from mundane
things?"

Let him who hopes for fame consider
   the extent of the starry skies
arching over our small planet.
   Can he think of shouting his name
and proclaiming his pride into the icy
   distances looming above him?
Does he rather wish to free
   his neck from mortality's yoke?

Will his name find a home in the mouths of
      strangers,
   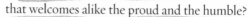and will death be at all impressed
that welcomes alike the proud and the humble?
      Where are Fabricius' bones
or those of Brutus or stern Cato?
      They are reduced now,
those glorious names, to anecdotes.
      What can we know of the dead?
And do you suppose you won't be forgotten
      or that fame will keep you alive
on the lips of men for even a moment?
      Your last day will take
even this hope from your unclenching
      hand in a second death.

VIII

"But do not suppose that I am altogether in opposi-
tion to Fortune. Sometimes she deserves men's respect and deference. But those are the times when
she is honest and candid and shows her true face. Do
you have any notion of what I'm saying? It may seem
counterintuitive, but it is nonetheless true, although
it sounds peculiar when one puts it bluntly into
words. The fact of the matter is that ill fortune is

better for men than good. When Fortune smiles, she is always false. But when she is inconstant and whimsical, she shows her true self. The first aspect of Fortune will deceive people, but the second is instructive. The first blinds while the second opens men's eyes to how fragile the happiness of mortals really is. The man who enjoys good fortune is driven frantic, running this way and that and trying to maintain what he has. The other is steady and, if he learns from his experience, even wise. Good fortune can lead men astray, deceiving them about what to expect from life and how to think of themselves. When Fortune is unkind, she draws men back to an understanding of what the world is like, and who their friends are. Surely, in your time of trouble, you must have learned who were your real friends. The honest ones have been winnowed out from that crowd of associates and companions, all of whom have deserted you. What would you have paid back then to know which were which and whom to trust? Here you are, complaining of the wealth that you have lost, and you fail to recognize the wealth you have gained—knowledge of your true friends."

The world rings its regular changes,
its elements reconciled
held in balance in their battle

by its immutable laws.
Phoebus comes on with rosy dawns
in his flying golden car,
and Phoebe brings the silver moon,
fulfilling Hesperus' promise.
The churning sea is confined to its bed
and the land keeps to its bounds,
for each is subject to a greater power
the other helps to enforce.
What governs earth and sea and sky
is nothing less than love,
whose tight rein if it ever slackened
would leave creation in chaos
of civil war's utter ruin.
Love binds people too,
in matrimony's sacred bonds
where chaste lovers are met,
and friends cement their trust and friendship.
How happy is mankind,
if the love that orders the stars above
rules, too, in your hearts.

BOOK III

I

She finished singing, and the melody hung in the air, its sweetness still in my ears, which were eager for more. I waited a bit and then thanked her. "What wonderful comfort you offer, with both your arguments and your poetry. You do revive me, so that I am no longer absolutely devastated by the blows of fortune but seem at least for the moment able to bear them. At any rate, I am no longer terrified by the prospect of your 'strong remedies,' whatever they are, but eager for you to administer them."

"I thought it might be so," she answered, "because you were so absorbed and attentive. I am happy to have brought you to this state of mind. The remedies, I must warn you, sting a little, but once you have absorbed them they do soothe. And you say you are eager. But if you knew where I was leading you, you would be, I think, even more eager."

"Where is that?" I asked her.

"To that true happiness your soul dreams of but

cannot see because your sight is distracted by images."

"Tell me. Show me. I am eager to know what true happiness is. I beg you, let us proceed."

"Yes, gladly. But first I shall try to explain a subject about which you have some knowledge so that, when you have seen that clearly, you will then turn your eyes elsewhere and will recognize the appearance of happiness."

Whoever cultivates a virgin field
must first clear away the brush and weeds, and cut
with a sickle the ferns and brambles to enable
Ceres to come with her seeds of nourishing grain.
The taste in the mouth of honey is sweeter by far
if it follows something bitter, and stars in the sky
are all the brighter after the dark storm clouds
have been blown away by a steady wind from the
south.
The morning star is a beacon that shines at dawn
to welcome the glory of Phoebus' shining steeds.
And you, too, must prepare yourself for change,
withdraw your neck from the yoke of your false
gods
and raise your head in order that truth may enter.

II

She stared for a moment at the ground and gathered her thoughts. Then she raised her face to look directly at mine. "What all men want, although they seek it by different routes and through different activities, is to be happy. That is the summum bonum, the supreme good, the one that leaves room for no others, for if there were anything further to want it could not be the highest good. Something beyond it or outside it would remain to be desired. So happiness is necessarily that state that is perfect and that includes within it everything a man could want. Now, all men strive for this condition, although they do so by various means. The desire for happiness is inborn, instinctive in the minds of men. But they are led astray by false ideas of the good.

"Some men, for instance, think that the highest good is to want nothing, so they work hard to pile up wealth. Others are sure that honor is the highest good and they exert themselves to be honored and respected by their fellow citizens in the hope of having titles and distinctions awarded to them. Still others think that the highest good is in having the greatest power, and these men either try to rule or attach themselves as closely as possible to those who do. Yet others think that fame is the summum bonum and they work to spread their names throughout the world either as warriors or statesmen. But most men think of the good as their allotment of joy and good spirits, and they abandon themselves to the pursuit of pleasure. There are also those who mix and match, going after wealth so that they can use it to pursue power, or they work for power to get rich or to increase their fame. You can see in how many different directions men scurry in the pursuit of what they think will bring them happiness. Men want rank in order to be famous; or they want a wife and children for the pleasures of family life; or they want friendship—which is not a gift of Fortune but of virtue. But almost anything else they want for the purposes of what it can do or how it can be pleasing.

"The good that can come from the body is related to these goals. With strength and size comes power; with beauty and speed comes fame; and from good health comes pleasure. But in every one of these things, it is happiness that men really want and that they reckon as the highest good. We have already defined the highest good as happiness. And each man simply assumes that what he happens to want more than anything else will bring him happiness.

"So here you have it, all laid out before you, all

those things that men think will make them happy: wealth, honor, power, fame, or voluptuary pleasure. Epicurus looked at this array and decided that pleasure was the highest good, since all the rest of them were merely mental. But I think that the mind is not to be so easily dismissed, and although it can sometimes be clouded and confused, still, what it wants is its proper good; but, like some drunk on his way home, it cannot remember which is the right path. Are those who are trying not to want for anything really wrong? It certainly is conducive to happiness to have plenty, to need no one's help, and to be entirely self-sufficient. Are those who want reverence and respect altogether wrong? The effort of men to obtain respect is by no means base or contemptible. Is power a bad thing? Surely, it is better than weakness. And is fame always bad? Nobody can argue that most things that are excellent are also famous. And it hardly needs to be said that happiness is not possible for one who is worried, or depressed, or afraid of pain or trouble.

"These are all things that men want—wealth, high office, power, fame, and pleasure—because these are the things they think will make them happy. The good, then, is that which men pursue by these various means and avenues. And we can look to nature

in admiration because, <u>although men have different</u>
<u>ideas about how to go about it, they are united in</u>
<u>their desire for the good.</u>"

With responsive strings, I sing of how
great Nature controls all things with her laws
and how she keeps track of the universe
with a steady attention that never flags
and looks after each tiny creature
held fast in necessity's net.
There are lions in Carthage held in chains
of fine-wrought gold that are trained to feed
from a man's hand, and they fear his beatings,
but once blood touches their huge jaws
they revert, go feral, break their bonds,
and turn on their master to slake their thirst
for blood and revenge from his torn flesh.
The bird that sang free in the treetops,
shut in a cage and turned into a toy,
drinks her honeyed food from her dish,
but let her, from the bars of that cage,
glimpse those treetops that used to be home,
and she will scatter her food and sulk,
twittering only songs of grieving
about those trees through which she once flew.
Take a sapling and tie its top
so that it is bowed down to the ground,

then cut the rope or let it give way
and the tree will point again to the sky.
Phoebus' car goes down in the west
but rises again in its regular place
in the east to usher in the morning.
Each thing seeks its own return
to what it knows as its preordained
course, so that endings often announce
new beginnings in ordered cycles.

III

"Earthly creatures that you are, you have some hazy idea of your beginning, some vague dream of it anyway, and you have a similarly unclear notion of that happiness that is your end and goal. Your natural inclinations draw you in that direction, toward the true good, but your mistaken ideas confuse you and lead in wrong directions. Just ask yourself if men can succeed in finding happiness through the means that they think will lead them there. If money or honors or any of those things produce a perfect happiness from which nothing is left to be desired, we would admit that some men at least are happy seeking those things, at least as the means to their end. But if they cannot perform as expected and promised and if they still leave one lacking in many things, isn't the appearance of happiness that they offer merely illusory? I ask you, who were rich at one time, whether that meant that you were never worried or anxious about something that could go wrong for you?"

"I can't remember a time when I wasn't worried, no."

"Was it because you thought something was missing? Or there was something present that you did not want?"

"Yes, both of those things."

"So you desired the presence of some things and the absence of others?"

"That's right."

"Now, everyone lacks something he desires, isn't that right?"

"Of course," I had to agree.

"But whoever lacks something is not completely self-sufficient."

"No, he couldn't be."

"And did you, loaded, as they say, wealthy as you were, feel this insufficiency?"

"Surely. Why not?"

"The point is that wealth doesn't make a man self-sufficient, or satisfied, even though this is what the idea of wealth seemed to promise. And then there is the consideration that there is nothing about having money that prevents its being taken away from those who have it."

"Yes, I'd have to agree to that."

"Of course you agree. Every day, somebody stronger takes wealth away from someone who is weaker. What else causes lawsuits? People are trying to get back what was taken away from them by force or trickery."

"Yes, that's true."

"So a man needs help, even from outside his family, to protect his money and keep it safe."

"That's true too."

"But if he didn't have any money, he wouldn't need protection because he wouldn't have anything to lose."

"There's a grim logic to that, yes."

"So it turns out that the opposite is true of what one might expect. Wealth was supposed to make a man self-sufficient, but it actually makes him dependent on the help of others. And anyway, money doesn't prevent a person from wanting. Rich men get hungry or thirsty, and rich men feel the winter's chill. Yes, yes, you will argue that rich men can buy food and drink and warm clothing, but all that means is that need is easier to deal with if one is rich. But even for them, need can't be erased or obliterated. Need is always there, grasping and demanding, and even with money it can never be satisfied. But nature is satisfied with relatively little, which is different from avarice, a kind of need that can never be met. Riches, then, don't remove need, but rather they produce a need of their own, for more and more. Why then would you believe that they can provide that self-sufficiency we were talking about?"

Let the rich man increase his hoard—it is never
        enough.
    All that gold, and all those Red Sea pearls
that hang from his pudgy neck, they only weigh
        him down.
    Out in his fields, hundreds of oxen plough,
but still the furrows of care are deep in his
        creased brow,
        and he worries about those riches he can't take
        with him.

IV

"Now," she said, "about high office, and the idea that it can bring honor and respect. Do you think for a minute that high offices fill the minds of those who hold them with virtue and drive away wickedness and venality? Isn't it the case that instead of reducing wickedness, high office makes it more notorious? It drives men into a frenzy to see this happen and they become indignant. Remember how Catullus called Nonius a "hairy wart" although he was sitting in the curule chair.* High office focuses attention on the defects of bad men that might otherwise have gone unnoticed. Could anyone have induced you to accept office with Decoratus, whom you know to be a villain and a clown as well as an informer? We cannot give respect to those in office if we know that the people are themselves unworthy. On the other hand, if you judged someone to be wise, you would respect him for his wisdom, wouldn't you? What we admire is virtue, and those in whom we find that virtue. The honors that the mob may give someone are no guarantee of that virtue. What do they know of virtue or beauty or the real worth of anything? Or look at it the other way around and figure that high office is less likely to occasion respect than hatred, because there are more people who look at them, know of their actions, and have reason to despise them. And the offices themselves come to be despised because the bad men who hold them defile them with their own taint.

"You will agree with me, I expect, that no one can

---

* Catullus 52.

earn respect from these shadowy dignities and titles. Let us suppose that a person who had held the consulship many times went to visit barbarians in the back of beyond. If the dignities had real value, they would go with him, just as fire takes its hotness with it no matter where it may be found. But respectability is not an inherent part of officeholding and is attributed to it only in the aberrant opinion of some men. Out there, among the barbarians who are too simple to share these false opinions, they see only the man and they don't pay any attention whatever to the titles he has or used to have. Those great titles don't even hold much weight here among the Romans who created these offices. Praetors used to have great power. Now it's a ceremonial job merely, and an expensive burden on the senatorial order. It used to be a great honor to be in charge of corn relief, but now it's a miserable job. There is nothing inherently grand about these positions, and therefore they vary in their respect and rank, depending on time and circumstance. They don't necessarily mean that the ones who hold them are particularly worthy, and they are respectable or not depending on who is in them or what the political weather may be. There is nothing in them to crave or hope for, either for yourself or for anyone else."

With fancy clothes, jewels, and gaudy badges,
>   Nero
> strutted along the streets, hated by all
who could see through all that fancy getup to his
>   mean heart,
>   shameless and, toward the end, probably crazy.
He foisted fools and villains upon the disgusted
>   Senate
> as consuls, but what did those empty honors
>   mean?

V

"But kings are happy, you think. It's good to be king, or at least to be close to a king. But there are stories, ancient and modern, of kings whose happiness turned to misfortune, and then you have to ask what good is that power if it isn't sufficient to protect itself. If this power over a kingdom were conducive to happiness, wouldn't any lack or defect in it be a cause of misery? And we know that any kingdom, however large, has a border beyond which that particular king does not rule. And wherever his rule ends, that is where his dissatisfaction begins as he realizes his limitation. So, if you think about it, kings have rather a larger share of misery than the rest of us. You recall how Dionysius I of Syracuse compared his position to that of Damocles with the sword hanging over his head. So what good is power if it is a source of constant worry and fear? Like any of the rest of us, kings would surely prefer to live out their lives without these kinds of worries, but they cannot. And they boast of their powers. But if you see a man who cannot accomplish what he wants to do, do you think of him as powerful? Is he powerful if he goes everywhere with bodyguards? Isn't he more afraid of others than they are of him? And that power depends, doesn't it, on a great horde of courtiers.

"If kings are not powerful, we hardly need describe those who are close to kings, who can be ruined either when the king is powerful or when he is overthrown. Nero forced Seneca, his old teacher and adviser, to commit suicide. Papinian had been powerful at court for a long time, but Caracalla had him executed. And each of these men was perfectly willing to step down and renounce his powers. Seneca even tried to give his wealth to Nero and go quietly into retirement. But they were standing on a height that turned out to be the brink of a precipice where they lost their footing, and neither one of them achieved what he had wanted. So again I ask what good is this power that causes men who have it to live in fear? When you want it you are not safe, and when you have it and want to get rid of it, you are also in peril. You can't trust your friends, who are drawn to you not by your virtue but only by your power and good fortune. And a man who is a friend to your good fortune will turn on you and let misfortune make you his enemy. And there is no enmity worse than that of an ex-friend."

He who hungers for power must learn
to tame that dangerous appetite;
he must never bend his neck to the heavy
yoke of that pernicious lust.
All India may quake at his name
and Ultima Thule forward its tribute,
but close at hand, by day and night,
misery and terror attend him
to mock both him and his powerless power.

VI

"And now we consider glory, which turns out to be deceptive and even vulgar. Euripides was on the mark when he said, 'O glory, glory, all those thou-

sands of mortals / that you have inflated to make
their lives seem great!"* How many men have ac-
quired their inflated reputations because of the
whimsical judgments of the mob—and what can be
more vulgar than that? There are those whose names
are in everybody's mouth, but they would blush to
hear what is being said. And even if the praise of the
crowd is in any way earned and justified, what does
the admiration of the rabble add to the self-esteem
of a wise man who does not pay attention to gossip
but knows in his own heart who and what he is? Or
turn the proposition around and ask whether, if it is
fair to have one's reputation spoken about by
everyone, then not to be talked about by all those
people is evidence of some kind of defect. And as we
have already agreed, there are people in distant cities
and countries who haven't been reached by this kind
of chatter and don't recognize any of Rome's great
men. Popular acclaim is not worth talking about. It
comes randomly, for little or no reason, and it never
lasts very long.

"And what a vain thing is nobility! If it comes
from fame, then it is a temporary nobility. And if
it comes from one's parents it is only borrowed.

---

* Euripides *Andromache* 319–320.

What it comes down to is that fame makes you famous, which is meaningless. If there is anything good at all to be said about nobility, it is that the nobles feel some slight obligation to behave well in order not to disgrace their prestigious ancestors."

All mankind comes from the same stock: you are children
of one father who rules over you all and cares
for all his sons and daughters. He gave you the horned moon;
he populated the earth with men; and he filled the skies
with shining stars. He also joined into their flesh
souls that deigned to descend from a home in the lofty heavens.
But if this was the noble origin of every mortal, why
should anyone boast of his forebears or his family's distinctions?
All of you can claim as ancestor and author
the God who made you—except for those who have turned away
to embrace sin and reject the gifts of their proper father.

VII

"Then there is the body and its pleasures, about which it is difficult to speak, for what do we have but the pains of longing followed by the regrets of satisfaction? One indulges the body and for this one gets pain and disease, which are difficult not to think of as the fruits of wickedness. What pleasure, then, is there is pursuing these kinds of indulgences, which so often have a bitter ending, as anyone knows who has any kind of memory? If bodily pleasure were the door to happiness, then beasts would be happy because they spend all their time and energy fulfilling their bodies' needs. There is pleasure a man gets from a wife and children, but as it has been said, children were invented to be our tormentors. Whatever their condition, we worry about them. As Euripides said, the childless are happy in their misfortune."*

Pleasures are alike, tormenting
those who pursue their sweetness.
Angry bees emerge from their hives
where the honeycombs were plundered
to swarm and inflict the sharp stings
of reproach on guilty hearts.

----

* Euripides *Andromache* 420.

VIII

"So all these paths that we think may lead to happiness are false trails and cannot take us to where we want to go. And as I shall demonstrate, they lead in wrong and even wicked directions. Do you want to pile up large sums of money? Where will you get it, if not from those who have it? You want honors? How will you obtain them except by begging for them from those who can bestow them, thereby becoming not the proud man you wanted to be but a suppliant, a mendicant? You want power? You will lie awake at night worrying about your subjects' treachery. You want glory and fame? You will be the toy of vicissitude, trying to figure out the mood of the people and drawn this way and that by their fickle preferences. You want pleasure? You become the servant of your body, which you know to be both frail and base. There are those who take pride in their bodies, but . . . why? What man can compare to an elephant in size? Or a bull in strength? Or a tiger in speed? Look up at the heavens and marvel at the steadiness and the speed of the stars and constellations and then think of the puniness of the human body. And what is impressive in the sky is not just the speed but the order, the regularity those bodies display. The human body can be beautiful, but its beauty passes like that of spring flowers. And think of Aristotle's observation that if we had the keenness of sight of Lynceus the Argonaut and could see through surfaces, the beauty even of an Alcibiades would be a disgusting heap of guts and organs. It isn't the human body, then, that is attractive, but only the weakness of human vision that makes it seem so. And anyway, however beautiful a human body may be, that beauty can be utterly destroyed in the course of a three-day fever. So we see that all these things do not provide the happiness they promise, nor can they lead us to any kind of perfection, singly or in combination. They cannot make men happy."

Alas, how blind are men who stumble
    along the wrong path!
They hope to find gold and jewels
    hanging in trees.
They cast their nets wide and fish
    on the mountaintops,
or they try to hunt for wild goats
    out on the sea.
Oh, they know where to dive for pearls
    and where the murex dwells,
the source of our precious purple dye.
    They can find shellfish

but they cannot begin to locate the good
  that looms high up
over the earth on which they tread.
  They are hopeless fools
in endless pursuit of money and fame.
  When they have reached
their worthless goals they will come to know
  how far they went wrong.

IX

Taking a breath and actually smiling at me, she then said, "I have said enough, I imagine, about false ideas of happiness. And if you have been following me and have understood my observations, then the next step is to show what true happiness is."

I was glad to hear this, and I reassured her. "I do see that sufficiency cannot be got through wealth or power or even kingship, or respect from office. I have seen the limitations of fame and of bodily pleasures."

"And you have understood the reasons for all this?"

"I have a glimpse," I said. "But I should be happy to have any further explanation."

"The explanation is this," she said. "What is simple and undivided by nature human error manages to divide and distort. What is true and perfect becomes false and imperfect. Do you suppose, for instance, that that which needs nothing is in need of power?"

"No, that can't be."

"You are correct. If it needs power, it needs the help of other people."

"Yes."

"So power and self-sufficiency turn out to be the same."

"That would follow."

"And would you consider a being of this kind, powerful and self-sufficient, contemptible or worthy of respect?"

"Worthy of respect, by all means."

"So we can add respect to the power and the self-sufficiency, isn't that right? All these three come together."

"Fine, we have all three together then."

"And do you think this condition we are describing is obscure and undistinguished? Or is it deserving of fame and renown? Would a state that lacks nothing and has power and honor be lacking in fame? Would it need that and therefore seem to be somehow deficient? Could it provide that for itself?"

"Being what it is," I said, "it would also be re-nowned."

"So fame is part of the package and goes with the other three."

"That would follow, too."

"And let us add one more quality, for that which is self-sufficient, powerful, famous, and worthy of re-spect would also be most happy, isn't that right?"

"I can't imagine how there could be, in that condi-tion, an occasion for sadness, assuming that all the other conditions remain with it."

"So what we get to is a condition in which the names of all those things—self-sufficiency, power, fame, respect, and pleasure—are different, but their substance is the same."

"That would have to be true."

"Now, this state, which is one and simple in its es-sence, is what men divide as they try, in their mis-guided way, to get a part of it, although in fact it has no divisible parts. Their mistake is not trying to ob-tain the whole thing."

"Tell me more," I asked her.

"Well, the man who is trying to escape neediness wants to be rich, but he doesn't give much thought to power. He prefers to be obscure and he denies him-self pleasures and indulgences so as not to lose any of the money he has managed to acquire. But in this way, he can't be happy, because he is powerless, vulnerable, abject, and obscure. Similarly, a man who wants only power squanders his wealth, and he doesn't care about fame, which he thinks is worthless. And sometimes he lacks the basic necessities of life. And he worries a lot, which means that he has lost the thing he was trying to gain, which was to be powerful. You can make the same argument about any of these aspects of happiness, for each one is like the others, in that it is, in isolation, inadequate. Whoever seeks one of these things apart from the others doesn't even get the one he was hoping for."

"But suppose that a man tried to seek them all together. Wouldn't he then be trying for the sum of happiness?"

"Do you think that he could find it among those things, each of which is unable to provide what it promises?"

"No, probably not."

"Then happiness is not to be sought in any of its individual aspects. Men are merely beguiled by these things."

"All right, I agree."

"Then you understand the forms of false happiness and their causes. But the time has come for you to turn your mind in the other direction, where you will find true happiness, as I promised you a while back."

"Excellent. And I see now that while you were explaining false happiness, you also made it clear that true happiness would be that which makes a man self-sufficient, powerful, respected, famous, and happy. Only that would be what we could call a full and true and perfect happiness. And all these, I have come to realize, are fundamentally the same."

"Very nearly perfect," she said. "All you need to be the ideal pupil is to add one thing."

"And what would that be?"

"Do you think that there is anything in this changeable and mortal world that can provide a condition such as you have described."

"Almost certainly not," I had to concede. "What you have been saying makes that so clear that no further argument or discussion is required."

"These things, we agree, seem to give men images of the good, or at least of certain imperfect goods, but they cannot lead to the true and perfect good."

"Quite right," I said.

"Then, since you have begun to understand what is true happiness and what are the things that merely counterfeit it, what now remains is for you to recognize where you can find this true happiness."

"That is exactly what I have been hoping for."

"You have read Plato, and you remember what he said in the *Timaeus,* which is that we ought to ask for God's help even in the smallest matters. What do you then suppose we should do now to make us worthy of discovering where that highest good may dwell?"

"We must call upon God for this, too," I said, "for if this is omitted, there cannot even be a first step that is proper and correct."

"Exactly so," she said. And she began to sing:

O Lord, you govern the universe with your
        eternal order:
you brought time itself into being, and all that
        marks
its changes in the heavens and here on the earth,
        both moving
and also in stillness. Nothing but your love could
        have prompted you
to bring forth the matter and forms that together
        make up the world.
From within yourself, ungrudging, you brought
        out the pattern of all
that is good, inasmuch as it partakes of your own
        goodness.
Its beauty is your beauty; your mind is the source
        of its grandeur
as you shaped it to your liking, imposing upon it
        your order,
which harmonizes the many elements that
        compose it,

the cold with the fiery hot, the dry with the wet,
    lest any
fly off on its own and unbalance the equipoise of
    creation.
You bound the Soul together in its intricate
    threefold structure
of Same, Other, and Being—the Soul that moves
    all things
in inevitable circles that mirror the orbits of
    heaven,
visible and beyond, with each man having his own
star to guide his journey, descending to earth and
    then
rising again at the end in its chariot headed home,
where the fire returns to the hearth from which it
    first set forth.
Grant me, o father, that gift by which my mind
    can rise
after its peregrination to the seat of your majesty,
and give me the light to behold through the thick
    clouds of our skies
a clearer heaven in which your brightness flashes
    forth.
To the blessed who alone behold it, you are the
    sole serene
goal in which we may rest, satisfied and tranquil,
and to see your face is our only hunger, our only
    thirst,

for you are our beginning, our journey, and
our end.

X

"And now," she said, "since you have seen what imperfect and perfect happiness are, I think it is time
to look at where the perfect happiness can be found.
The question is whether the perfect good, as we have
defined it, can exist in this world. At the least, this
will prevent us from wasting time looking for some
will-o'-the-wisp or being deceived by empty fanta-
sies. But that the perfect good, the source of all good,
exists is impossible to deny. Anything that is imperfect is imperfect because it is lacking in some way
and falls short of perfection. Thus, we can reason
that if there is a class of things in which there are im-
perfections, there must also be in that class the perfect thing. Without that perfect thing, it cannot even
be imagined how the imperfect ones could exist. The
universe did not begin with diminished, unfinished,
and imperfect things, but began with perfections
from which it lapsed into the present diminished
and exhausted state. So, if there is a certain imperfect happiness in a good that is not lasting and complete, it follows that there must also be some endur-
ing and perfect happiness."

"I can see the necessity of that line of reasoning," I said.

"And if we want to know where that can be found," she said, "we must think in this way. We can demonstrate that God is good by looking at how men conceive of God—than whom nothing can be better. This means that God is not only good but that the good in him is a perfect good. If it weren't, then there would be something better than God, something more excellent than he is. But it is by definition that perfect things are better than whatever is less than perfect. And to avoid having our argument fall into an infinite regression, we can state that the most high God is full of the most high—which is to say the perfect—good."

"I see no flaw in that argument nor any way to contradict it."

"And do you understand fully the implications of what you've just agreed to, about the most high God being filled with the perfect good?"

"What do you mean?"

"Where does that highest good come from? Does the Father of all things receive it from outside, or is it from within, the substance of happiness being the same as his own substance? This is important because if God were to receive this higher good from some external source, then that source would be more excellent than he, who merely receives it. But that can't be, because he is the most excellent of all things. And if it is from within him but its essence and his own are different, then, since we are talking about the author of all things, we cannot conceive of who might have joined these two distinguishable substances together. And if they were distinguishable, then that would mean that God is not, in himself, the highest good, which would be a wicked thought, and it would also contradict what we agreed before, which is that there is nothing more excellent than he. There is no question, then, but that the author of all things is inherently and in his substance the highest good."

"Absolutely," I agreed.

"And we said earlier that the highest good is happiness."

"Yes, we did."

"Then happiness is itself God."

"That is where the propositions lead us. I don't see any wiggle room."

"It confirms what we have been saying to consider how there cannot be two highest goods that are different from one another. For if they are different, then they are not the same, and if one is higher than the other, then they are not both the highest. In fact, neither would be perfect because each would be lacking the other. And what is not perfect would not be that summum bonum. Therefore, both God and happiness are the highest good, which would have to be the nature of the highest divinity."

"It has the logic of a geometric theorem," I conceded.

"And just as geometricians can draw corollaries from their theorems, so there is a corollary that can be drawn here. Since men want happiness, and since happiness is in itself divinity, then it follows that men in the pursuit of happiness are actually in the pursuit of divinity. But as in their efforts to pursue justice they become just, and in the pursuit of wisdom they become wise, this logic would lead us to conclude that in the pursuit of divinity they would become gods, which is awkward because God, by his nature, is singular. Still, there is nothing that prevents the acquisition of divinity by participation in his divinity."

"Whether or not it's a corollary, that's wonderful! Beautiful!"

"But the most beautiful thing is where this line of reasoning leads."

"And where is that?" I asked.

"We have to ask whether all things that we include under the heading of happiness are like parts that combine to form a single body but still with a definable separateness, or is there one of them that is the essence of happiness which includes all the others in a subordinate way."

"I'm not quite sure that I follow."

"We think of happiness as something good, don't we?"

"Yes, of course. The highest good."

"So each of these things in its perfection would be an aspect of happiness: absolute self-sufficiency, for instance, would be the same as happiness; and the highest power and the highest respect and the highest fame and pleasure would all be the same as happiness? The question is whether all these good things are members of a body, or is goodness a category to which they all belong?"

"I think I understand the question. But what would your answer be?"

"I would resolve the problem by saying that if each of these were related to happiness as limbs are related to a body, they would differ from one another, because the body is one but the parts of it are diverse. But we have shown that all these things are identical, and therefore they can't be like limbs. Or happiness would be a body made up of a single limb—which is silly."

"Fine. I'm with you that far. What comes next?"

"Each of these things is classed as a good, and people want them because they believe them to be good and therefore desirable. This is true of power, or fame, or pleasure, or any of those things we have been talking about. But in all cases, what men are seeking is goodness. What is not good, or is not perceived to be good, is not something that men want. But there are things that are not good but seem good, or are thought to be good, and men do pursue those. But in every case, what men want is goodness.

"Suppose a man wants to go horseback riding for the sake of his health. It isn't the actual experience of riding and the motion of the horse that he desires but the effect, which is health. It is like that with all things that men want, in which they are not so much interested in the things but in their goodness. And we have agreed that what men want is happiness, and in the same way, when they pursue various goals for the purpose of achieving happiness, it is the happiness that they want. It would appear, then, that goodness and happiness are one and the same."

"I can't imagine any objection to that."

"And we have shown that God and happiness are the same thing."

"Yes."

"So we may conclude that the substance of God is goodness itself, which can be found nowhere else."

Come out, you prisoners, loosed from your chains
    and shame,
come out together, into the light and air,

freed from the bonds of desire. Here find rest
and a refuge at last from the pain of your
            unremitting
labors, the only sanctuary there is.
The Tagus to the west and the eastern Hermus,
rich with their nuggets of gold, and the southern
            Indus,
where emeralds lie in the mud to gleam in your
            dreams,
offer you nothing after all but blindness.
The riches are elsewhere, and the glorious
            shining
you search for is not to be found in the earth's
            caves.
The grandeur of heaven eludes the corrupted
            soul,
and only those who can see with their eyes and
            their minds
can observe this light, brighter than any sun.

XI

"It all holds together logically," I said, "and I agree
entirely."

"And if you come to know what the good itself is,"
she asked, "how highly will you value it?"

"Infinitely," I replied at once, "for then I should come to know God, who is himself the good."

"I shall make that clear too with the use of reason, building upon the foundations we have already established."

"We have, indeed," I volunteered, eager for her to continue.

"We have agreed that the things most men seek are not true and perfect goods because they differ from one another and therefore each is incomplete, because any one of them lacks the others, and therefore none can be the total and absolute good. On the other hand, true good includes all the goods gathered together into one form, which, as a sufficient cause, produces a sufficiency which is identical to and includes power, respect, fear, pleasure, and the rest. But unless they are all the same, they are not worth pursuing."

"You have explained that and your reasoning seems perfectly sound."

"When we consider all these things that are not good because they differ but become good when they merge into one, does it not seem that they become good because they approach this unity?"

"It would seem so, yes."

"Then we can infer that the one and the good are the same. Those things that are truly good have the same substance, the effect of which, because of their nature, is the same."

"That would follow."

"And you also know that everything that exists endures and perseveres as long as it is a unity but is destroyed as soon as it ceases to be a unity."

"I don't quite see that. Can you explain it more?"

"In a living thing, for instance, while the body and soul are united and remain together, the result is alive, but if body and soul are separated, the creature perishes and is no longer a living thing. And the body itself, so long as all the parts are united and it remains in one form, continues as a human being, but if the parts are separated or torn apart, then it stops being what it was. This is true and obvious about all living organisms."

"Yes, I see now, and I can think of many more examples."

"Fine, but then ask yourself if there is any living thing that, if it is acting naturally, abandons its appetite for existence and survival and wants its own destruction and corruption?"

"Among living things that have what we could call a preference or a will and can want or not want this or that, I can't think of anything that, without some outside influence, is likely to stop trying to remain alive and would hurry toward its own destruction.

Every animal at least tries to protect itself and to avoid death and destruction. About plants or trees or things that are in no way alive, I'm not so sure."

"No, no, if you think about plants and trees, you see that they grow in places that are suitable for them where, insofar as nature allows, they can grow and thrive and avoid withering and dying. Some plants grow in fields and others on mountains, or in marshes, and some cling to stones, and some grow in the barren sands—and if they were transplanted to a place you or I would think of as likelier for vegetation, they would die. Nature gives each plant what is appropriate for it and keeps it alive as long as possible. You must have observed how they stand there in the ground with their roots acting as mouths with which they eat and drink and supply themselves with nourishment that they draw up to their bark and their pith. And you will have also observed that the soft pith is protected by a harder outer bark that shields them against severe weather and other kinds of threats. And think how well nature tends to the plants, propagating them by means of their seeds, which are the mechanism for their survival from one generation to the next. And as to things that are not alive, they too have mechanisms for persisting. There is the lightness of flame that carries it upwards, and there is the heaviness of earth that weighs it down, and these different motions are appropriate and fitting for each substance. And it is this appropriateness that allows each substance to survive and persist, whatever it is. Hard things like stones hold tightly together and resist being broken up, while flowing things, like air or water, yield easily to whatever divides them and then flow together again. And fire avoids any division whatsoever.

"We are talking here not of voluntary motions of intelligent souls but of the workings of nature, in which we also participate. We digest the food we have consumed without any conscious thought and we breathe in our sleep without being aware of what we are doing. Even in living things, then, the love of survival is not something that is willed but a consequence of natural principles. Indeed, there are times when the will may decide it is better to die, while nature fears and avoids death. Or although nature always wants it, there may be occasions when the will decides to refrain from the act of procreation that perpetuates all mortal things. You see, then, that this love of self comes not from the will but from nature, as a gift of providence, so that all things desire to persist and endure for as long as they can. So there is nothing that could cause you to doubt that things naturally desire to survive and to avoid destruction."

"I didn't quite see that, I confess, but I am now persuaded," I told her.

"And whatever desires to endure also desires to be one, for if unity is lost then there won't be anything that can continue."

"That follows," I conceded.

"You agree that all things desire unity."

"Yes."

"And we have already agreed that unity is the same thing as the good."

"Yes, we have."

"Therefore, all things seek the good. Or, to put it another way, the good is the goal of all things."

"That is true, for either all things are unrelated and left without any shared goal, or, if there is anything toward which all things tend, it would have to be the highest good."

"Splendid. You are an excellent pupil, for you have hit the mark exactly and arrived at the heart of the truth. What you have just said is something you had not known before."

"What was that?"

"The end and object of all things," she answered. "For all things desire the good, and the good is the goal and end of everything."

Whoever with profound contemplation seeks
the truth and wants to avoid misleading paths
must turn his vision inward, so that his quest
may circle back, and, instead of wandering far,

seek that treasure stored in his own heart.
What error's dark clouds had covered over
will then blaze forth with Apollo's own
    brightness.
That light of the mind was never altogether
dimmed by the heavy flesh that causes men
to forget the seeds of truth that were never lost
and that teaching can revive to blossom again.
How else can it be that, when you are asked a
    question,
something deep within you answers correctly
unless those seeds remained there? Plato's muse
tells us the secret: those things men once knew
and thought that they had lost can be
    remembered.

XII

After a moment, I said, "I am very much in agree-
ment with Plato. You have reminded me twice now
of his teachings. You spoke of what my memory lost
because of the contamination of my body. And now
you have shown me that, because I had lost that
memory, I was overwhelmed by grief."

"If you think about those things we have agreed
on," she answered, "you will be on the verge of re-

membering what you said a little while ago you did not know."

"And what was that?" I asked.

"How the universe is governed."

"I do remember saying that I didn't understand that. And I can see glimmers of an idea, but I'd appreciate it if you could tell me a bit more."

"You said some time ago that you thought the universe is ruled by God."

"Yes, and I think that is beyond question. With your indulgence, I shall review the arguments by which I came to that position. It seemed to me that the universe is composed of so many different parts that it could never have come together unless there was one to join all these elements. All these diverse and even contrary pieces would fly apart if there was not one who held together what he had originally conjoined. Without God, there could not be so orderly a series of natural processes with intricate motions in place and time, unless there was one who imposed and maintained this order. And whatever it is that created and maintains the universe I call by the name of God."

"Very good," she answered. "And if this is what you think, we have only a little further to go for you to return safely to your homeland, where you can grasp that happiness you have been looking for. You

remember, of course, that one of the requisite qualities of happiness was self-sufficiency, and we decided
that God was happiness itself."

"Yes, both of those things are correct."

"So we can infer that God needs no outside help
in ruling the universe because, if he did, he would
not have full self-sufficiency."

"That's logical."

"Therefore, he alone orders all things."

"One cannot deny that."

"And we have seen that God is goodness itself."

"We did, indeed."

"So he orders all things for the good, inasmuch as
he orders all things and he is good. This is the tiller
and the rudder by which the universe is preserved
and kept safe."

"I agree, and I even knew that you would be saying something like that."

"Yes, I am not surprised, because you have trained
your eyes better to see the truth. And what I am
about to say will also seem clear to you, I believe."

"And what is that?"

"Inasmuch as God is correctly believed to order all
things at the helm of goodness, and all those things,
on their own, aspire toward the good by their natural inclination, can there be any question about their
voluntary submission to God's rule and obedience to

his commands? After all, that is their disposition anyway."

"It must be so," I said. And his rule would not be happy if he were subjecting unwilling creatures to the yoke of obedience rather than imposing it upon those who are willingly inclined that way."

"So there is nothing that, in the effort to remain true to its nature, would want to try to oppose God?"

"No, nothing," I said.

"But if something were to try, then, because God is all-powerful, would it be in any way successful?"

"It couldn't possibly succeed or achieve anything at all."

"So there is nothing that would or could oppose the highest good."

"I can't see how, no."

"It is, then, the highest good that rules things firmly but in a kindly way and orders them well."

"This is a very soothing idea, and I delight in the words you use. I am ashamed of the folly of my misery."

"You have read the stories of the giants challenging heaven. But they were put in their place in a strong but gentle way. It might be a way of testing our logic to consider these stories and to see if some spark of truth flies up from the collision."

"Whatever you like."

"No one would question the idea that God has power over all things."

"No sane person could have any doubt."

"And there is nothing that God can't do, being omnipotent."

"No, there is nothing he can't do."

"But God cannot do evil, can he?" she asked.

"No, I suppose not."

"Then evil is nothing, because God cannot do it, and there is nothing he cannot do."

"Is that a serious statement, or are you playing logical games with me?" I asked. "It's a labyrinth, and you manage to go in where you are going to come out, or you go out where you came in. Or are you deliberately making it all a circle that demonstrates the simplicity of God? A while ago, you said that happiness was the highest good, and you placed that in God, and argued that God was the highest good and complete happiness, and where we came out was that no one could be happy unless he was also a god. Then we talked about the substance of God and of happiness and we worked it out that unity was the same thing as the good, which was what the entire natural world aspired to. And you argued that God ruled the universe with the tiller of goodness, and that all things voluntarily obeyed him. And then we get to the place where evil doesn't exist? This involves no external proofs and demonstrations but is internally consistent with arguments each one of which validates the others."

"No, it is not a game," she said, quite soberly. "We have looked at the most important of all subjects with the help of God, to whom we prayed at the beginning of our talk. For the form of divine substance is such that it does not devolve into external things, nor does it receive anything from external sources. Instead, it is, as Parmenides says, 'like the mass of a sphere, rounded on all sides.' It is the unmoving pivot on which the world turns. But if you are worrying about a lack of external reference, you should take comfort from Plato, who tells us that words refer to the real things that they designate."

Happy is he who is able
to find the fountain of goodness,
and happy, too, is he
who can free himself from the chains
that bind him to heavy earth.
Orpheus long ago sang
his dirge for Euridyce's death
and rooted trees ran to hear
and running rivers stopped
to listen. The hind lay down

with the savage lion in safety,
and the hare and the coursing hound,
were rapt and at peace together
in the notes of his mournful threne
that soothed every heart that heard it—
but not that of the singer,
whose grief burned all the more fiercely,
and, wailing, he raged at the gods.
He dared to venture below
where his lyre's music echoed
that he drew from his instrument
and the gifts of his mother, the muse,
as he sang of his loss that his love
made only the harder to bear.
The dead quickened with feeling
the griefs of his sweet singing
as he made his plea to the gloomy
lords of the underworld
and begged that they might relent.
The three-headed dog at the gate
fell utterly silent, enchanted.
The Furies who terrify
the souls of the guilty melted
and tears coursed down their cheeks.
Ixion at his turning
wheel stopped for the moment,
and Tantalus, tormented,

paused in his quest for water.
Even the vulture ceased
to tear at Tityus' liver.
Hades himself announced:
"We grant this man his wife,
bought by his wonderful singing.
But the terms of the gift are these—
that as he is leaving our realm
he may not look back or look down."
But who can give rules to lovers?
The heart makes its own decrees.
Alas, alas! At the very
verge of the dark kingdom,
Orpheus had his moment
of doubt, and turned and saw,
and lost the woman forever.
This old and familiar tale
is yours, as you make your ascent
leading your mind to the light,
for if, in a moment of weakness,
you should look back on the darkness,
the excellence you have achieved
you will lose, looking back, looking down.

BOOK IV

I

When Philosophy had finished singing these grace-
ful verses, she looked at me with a serious face and
seemed to be about to speak, but I had not altogether
forgotten my troubles and, before she could begin, I
asked her a question. "Lady," I said, "what you have
said so far is inspiring, divinely inspired, and most
plausible in its logic. You have reminded me of things
I had forgotten because of my injuries and reverses,
although I probably did have some vague recollection of them. But it remains true, and is the cause of
my distress, that even though there is a ruler of the
universe who is good, there is nonetheless evil in the
world, even evil that passes unpunished. I beg you to
address yourself to this knotty question, which causes
so much wonder among men. And there is a further
question, too, which is that when wickedness rules,
virtue not only goes unrewarded but is even overthrown and trodden under the feet of bad men. Virtue pays the penalty, rather than vice. That this can

happen in the kingdom of God, who knows all and is all-powerful, and who wills only the good, is something no man can either wonder at or complain about."

"It is, indeed, a difficult problem, more frightening, really, than any evil omen could be. It is as if, in a well-run household of so great a master, the worthless goblets and platters were cherished while the valuable ones were carelessly looked after and had become filthy. But it doesn't happen that way. We had agreed that with the help of that God we were talking about, the good are always powerful while the wicked are abject and weak. Vices are never unpunished and virtue is never unrewarded. This observation will solve your problems and corroborate your reasoning. I have shown you, and you have seen, the condition of true blessedness. And you recognized where it can be found. When we have reviewed these matters, I shall show you the way home, and your mind will have wings to carry it aloft so that, untroubled, you can return home under my guidance, on my path, and in my carriage."

Philosophy has wings with which you can fly,
        ascending
    as an exaltation of larks to heaven,

and when your mind has fastened them on and
    soared,
    it can look down on the earth with contempt.
Flying even higher beyond the spheres
    of air, it can look below at the clouds
and climb beyond the highest point of fire,
    rising even to the house of the stars
to the path where Phoebus makes his daily
    passage
    or join with ancient Saturn as page
in his army of stars that spangle the night skies.
    Having thus achieved, it then
can aspire even further, beyond the upper
    air toward the awesome dazzling light
where the king of kings wields his royal scepter
    and holds the reins that control the world.
He guides his chariot, although he does not move,
    the effulgent universal master.
There you will at last remember yourself,
    on the road back, the road home,
and you will say, "Yes, I recall it all,
    where I was born, where I belong.
Here I shall stay!" And should you chance to look
    down
    to the dark earth you have left behind,
where wretched people fear their tyrant rulers,
    you shall see them all as exiles.

II

"Splendid!" I exclaimed. "What magnificent promises. And I have no doubt about your fulfilling them. But let us proceed. I am eager, believe me."

"The propositions that good men are powerful and that wicked men are weak are derived from what we have agreed upon already. And in fact each of them proves the other, because good and evil are contraries, and if we establish that goodness is powerful, then it must follow that wickedness is weak. Or, turning it around, if we establish that evil is weak, then good must logically be strong. But so that you may trust what I am saying, I shall go about the proof from both directions, and show you that no matter where we begin, we come out with the same conclusion.

"Any human action presupposes two things: will and ability. If either one of these is lacking, no one can do anything. Without the will, no man can begin any action, and without ability, the will is frustrated. So if you see someone who wanted to obtain something and failed to do so, you would conclude that he lacked the ability to get what he wanted."

"That sounds reasonable. I can't see anything to object to."

"And the converse would be that with the man

who has achieved what he set out to do there can be no doubt that he was able to do it."

"None whatever."

"So every man should be judged strong in what he is able to do and weak in what he is not able to do."

"That sounds right."

"You remember what we agreed on before, that the whole effort of man's will, which is vital in his activities, is in the direction of happiness?"

"Yes, we agreed to that idea."

"And you remember, too, that happiness is the good itself. And that men who seek happiness are seeking the good."

"I don't have to recall that. It has remained clear in my mind."

"All men, then, both good and evil, are making the same effort, which is to arrive at the good."

"That's true."

"And we cannot doubt that men become good by obtaining the good."

"That's true, too."

"And the good obtain what they are seeking."

"So it would appear."

"And if evil men obtained what they are seeking, which is to say the good, then they would not be evil."

"This is impossible to argue with."

"But since they are both seeking the good, but the good obtain it while the wicked do not, can there be any doubt that the good are powerful and the evil are weak?"

"This is where our argument leads us, I must admit."

"Now, let us suppose two men, both of them trying to perform the same action. One of them performs and completes the action in the normal way, but the other cannot function normally, but only tries to imitate the first man, who has succeeded. Which would you say is the stronger?"

"I know what you want me to say, but it's still murky to me. Can you be clearer?"

"Let us say that walking is a natural action."

"Yes, of course."

"Walking is a natural function of the feet."

"Quite true."

"Then let us suppose that one man is walking using his feet, while the other who lacked the proper use of his feet tried to walk on his hands. Which of these would you think is stronger?"

"That's ludicrous. The man walking on his feet is the stronger."

"Very well, then. The highest good, which is available to both the good and the wicked, the good try to get by the exercise of their virtues. But the wicked try to get it by the whims of their desires—which is not at all the natural way to obtain the good. Or do you disagree?"

"No, not at all. And what follows is also clear: the conclusion is inescapable that the good are strong and the evil are weak."

"You are getting the idea and I am delighted to see how you run with it. If I were a physician, I'd call that an excellent sign of your returning strength. And now that I see how receptive you are, I shall offer a number of arguments that all relate to one another. See how weak corrupt men are, who cannot even get what their natural inclination inclines them toward. What would it be like if they were deserted by this instinct and did not have nature to lead the way? Just consider how impotent they are! Those things they want and cannot get are by no means trifles or toys. Where they fail is in the most important thing in life, which they never achieve, even though they spend their days and nights striving for it. And it is in this light that the strength of the virtuous is demonstrably clear. Just as you would give the nod for strength to the man who could walk on foot to reach a place so distant that there was no further passage beyond it, so you must judge as the strongest that man who can attain the end of all de-

sirable things, beyond which there is nothing. And
on the other side, we have wicked men who are des-
titute of all power—for why do they abandon virtue
and pursue vice? Is it because they have no idea what
things are good? But what is weaker than the blindness of ignorance? Or do they know what is good
but nevertheless pursue those things for which they
have an uncontrollable desire? In this way, too, they
are weak because they do not have self-control
and are unable to fight against vice. Or is it know-
ingly and willfully that they abandon the good and
turn to vice? In this case, they are not merely powerless but they cease to exist, for those who do not
pursue the end of all things may be said to have
abandoned being.

"It seems puzzling, perhaps, to say that we should
say of evil men—who are the majority of mankind—
that they do not exist. But that is how it is. The evil
are, indeed, evil, and I can't deny that, but I do deny
that they are purely and simply evil. You would say of
a corpse, for instance, that it was a dead man, but you
could not call it simply a man. And for evil men, the
same thing holds, that they are evil, but not simply
evil. Those things exist that maintain their order and
nature, and whatever falls away from this abandons
its existence, which depends on its nature. You might
argue that evil men are still able to do things, and I

don't deny that, but this ability of theirs comes not from their strength but from their weakness. They could not do evil things if they had kept the power to do good. And the power that they do display demonstrates very clearly that they can really do nothing at all, for we agreed a while back that evil is nothing, and since they can only do evil, they can do nothing."

"That is clear enough."

"And to understand the nature of their power, you must remember that we have agreed that there is nothing more powerful than the highest good."

"Yes, we did agree to that."

"But the highest good cannot do evil."

"No, of course not."

"Now, does anyone suppose that men can do all things?"

"No one in his right mind thinks that, no."

"But still men do evil."

"It would be better if they couldn't," I observed.

"Now, then, a power that can only do good is omnipotent, but human beings, who can also do evil, are not. And those human beings who can do evil are less powerful. And we have also agreed that all forms of power are desirable and worth pursuing, and that these objects of desire are related to the good, as it were, to the very summit of their nature. But the ability to do evil cannot possibly be related to the good, and therefore it is not something to be desired. Power—all power—is desirable. So it is clear that the ability to do evil is not a power. And from this we can see the power of good men and the weakness of evil men, both of which are plain. And we can also see the truth of what Plato says in the *Gorgias* that only wise men can do what they desire, and that wicked men can do what pleases them but that that will not get them what they desire. They do whatever they want, believing that through those things that they enjoy they will achieve the good they desire. But they can never attain that good, because wicked deeds do not lead to happiness."

You can see those mighty kings sitting in state on
    their thrones,
robed in luxurious purple, surrounded by
    glittering armor,
their faces stern, their hearts filled with burning
    rage,
but only take away their raiment of vain splendor
and you will discern the festoons of heavy chains
    that bind them.
See the lust in their hearts, and observe their
    poisonous greed.
Note their anger that scourges their minds like a
    mighty whirlwind

lashing the waves of the sea. Their sorrows gnaw
    within them,
and their boundless hopes torment them,
    helpless and wretched victims.
The kings are overthrown; the rulers are ruled by
    these masters.

III

"Do you understand, then, in what a hog-wallow
wickedness finds itself, and with what brilliance
goodness shines? We can declare confidently that
good deeds never go unrewarded and that wicked
deeds never go unpunished. In every action, the result of the action is its reward. If we were talking of a
race, the crown of victory is clearly the reward for
the winner. But as we have agreed, happiness is the
good itself, that goodness for which all actions are
performed. Thus, goodness is the common reward

for all of men's actions. And it makes no sense to
separate goodness from good men, for those who are
deficient in goodness can no longer be called good.
However much the wicked may complain about it,
the wise man's laurels will not wither. Nor can one
wicked man filch the glory from one who is good.
That kind of borrowed glory can be taken away by

anyone, including him from whom it was borrowed. Glory, rather, is conferred on each man by his own goodness, and he loses his reward when he stops being good. Finally, inasmuch as every reward is desired because it is perceived to be good, who can say that someone who possesses the good is without his reward? What reward, after all?

For goodness = happiness!

"The greatest and the best! Remember that corollary we talked of earlier, in which we found that the good itself is happiness. It follows from that that all men are happy insofar as they are good. And those who are happy are divine. And that is the reward of good men, which time cannot diminish, no one's power can lessen, and no wickedness can hide—to become divine. If this is so for good men, what sensible person can doubt that punishment is inseparable from evil. Good and evil are opposites of one another, as punishments and rewards are opposites. And what we see in the necessity of the good man's reward must necessarily be the opposite, so that there is also necessity in the punishment of the wicked. Goodness is the reward of the good as wickedness is the reward of the wicked. It stands to reason that whoever is punished realizes that he is afflicted by something bad. So how could those men not think they were being punished, as their wickedness not only affects them but infects them?

How do wicked not realize their punishment?

"If wickedness is the opposite of the good, think how punishment hounds the wicked. We agreed before that everything that exists is unitary, and that oneness itself is good. It then follows that everything, because it exists, is good. And it also follows that whatever falls from goodness ceases to exist, and that evil men cease to be what they were, having by their wickedness lost their human nature, although they still survive in the form of the human body. It is goodness that raises a man above the level of humankind, and it therefore follows that evil thrusts a man down below the human condition, so that he no longer deserves the name of man. One given over to vice is therefore no longer to be deemed a man. One who plunders others' wealth is burning with avarice, and you could say that he is now a wolf. The wild one who is given to quarrels and lawsuits you could call a dog. The trickster with his cons and scams is a fox. The angry one who roars and cannot govern his anger is a lion. The coward who is afraid of everything is a deer. The stupid oaf is a jackass. The fickle one who follows his whims is a flighty bird. A man wallowing in his lusts is a pig. All those who have put goodness aside have no right to be called men anymore, since there is nothing divine about them, but they have descended to the level of beasts."

The Ithacan's black ship
and the rest of his wandering fleet
the winds drove to the island
where the fair goddess dwells,
the Sun's and Perse's daughter,
who serves each of her guests
in an enchanted cup
a brew she concocts herself
that changes them into beasts.
One turns into a boar,
another becomes a lion
with fangs and deadly claws,
and another is transformed
into the shape of a wolf
that cannot weep but howls
in his shame and his chagrin.
Another turns into a tiger
and paces about the villa
tame but mystified.
Mercury had pity,
but only on the captain,
and protected him from the poison
Circe had on offer.
His crew, nevertheless,
had already drained the potion
and, no longer men but swine,

rooted about for acorns,
their food now rather than bread.
Their voices were gone and their bodies
were altogether transformed.
Only their minds persisted
to recognize their disaster
and grieve at their dreadful fate.
That was the limit of Circe's
power and what her herbs
could do to these men: their bodies'
forms could change, but their hearts
stayed safe in an inner fortress
where the strength of man lies hidden.
Those poisons are much more toxic
that creep within and infect
the mind and the soul, while they leave
the outer shell untouched.

Dang'a

IV

Then from me: "Fine, I can see that and I understand that wicked men are mental beasts in human
bodies. But I do wish that those with such minds as
want to destroy the good didn't have the power to
achieve their aims."

"They don't," she replied, "as I shall demonstrate

to you later on. But let me remark now that if the power that is believed to be theirs were taken away, the burden of their punishment, to a great degree, would also be removed. You must understand that the wicked are all the more unhappy as their desires are fulfilled. If it is wretched to have evil desires, it is even worse to have the ability to carry them out. There are different levels of misery for people who have the desire to do something wicked, the power to do it, and the achievement of having done it, and these people suffer a triple misfortune."

"I wouldn't mind their losing that misfortune if they also lost the power to do evil," I observed.

"They will lose it, faster than you want and certainly faster than they expect. In the short span of a man's life, nothing is so far off as to seem long to wait for. All their direst plots and schemes suddenly collapse, often without any warning, and that sets a limit to their misery. If wickedness is a cause of their suffering, it would follow that their wickedness makes them unhappier the longer it lasts. If death did not end their evil, I would judge them the most unfortunate of men, for if suffering is a result of evildoing, then, if their evildoing were endless, their suffering would be infinite and eternal."

"It is an odd conclusion," I said, "and rather counterintuitive, but I admit that it is consistent with what we have agreed upon before."

"Your reasoning is correct. But if the conclusion is uncomfortable, then it is up to you to demonstrate either that some premise is false or that the logic does not lead to the uncomfortable conclusion. Otherwise, if the premises are accepted, there is absolutely no ground for objection. What I am about to tell you may seem just as counterintuitive, but it follows just as inevitably from the things we have already agreed are true."

"And what could that be?" I asked.

"That the wicked are actually happier being punished than they would be if there were no retribution to restrain them. I don't mean simply that bad behavior is corrected by retribution and the fear of punishment keeps people on the right path, or that the punishment of the wicked is an instructive example for others to keep them from straying and avoid evil. That is more or less obvious to anyone. But there is another way in which the wicked are more wretched if they are unpunished, even without the ideas of constraint or the example that punishment offers to others."

"And what is that other way?" I asked.

"We have agreed that the good are happy and the wicked are miserable, have we not?"

"Yes, we have."

"Now, if we added some good to someone's misery, would he not be happier than he would be if his misery were pure and unadulterated with any goodness?"

"I guess he would have to be," I answered.

"Now, let us suppose that for someone who is suffering and lacks every good another evil is added to his burden. He would then be even unhappier than someone whose pain is lessened by some share of the good, wouldn't he?"

"That would follow, yes."

"But clearly it is just for the wicked to be punished and unjust for them to evade punishment."

"No argument there."

"And there can be no argument either about the proposition that everything that is just is good, and on the other hand everything that is unjust is evil."

"Certainly."

"Then the wicked, as they are being punished, have some goodness added to them—the punishment itself, which is just and therefore good. And by the same token, if they go unpunished, that is an injustice, which is a further evil."

"I can see no fault in the logic of that argument."

"Therefore, the wicked who evade or avoid punishment are less happy than those who are justly punished."

"That, too, is logical. But let me ask if you think

there are punishments for the soul after the death of the body."

"Yes, there are, some of them extremely harsh, and some, I think, with a purifying mercy. But that is not the subject I want to discuss just now. What I am trying to do at the moment is to get you to recognize that that the power of the wicked, to which you just made objection, is really nothing. And I want you to understand that those who are unpunished do not actually escape from paying the penalty for their wickedness. That license they have to do evil does not last very long. And if it lasted longer, the evil-doers would be even unhappier. And if it were eternal, they would be infinitely miserable. Finally, the wicked who escape punishment are more unhappy than if they are punished with a just and proper penalty. They are burdened with an even greater punishment just when they think they have got off scot-free."

"Your argument holds together perfectly well, but if you were to go out into the streets and talk with ordinary people, I'm not sure that you could get them to agree with you, or even listen with a straight face."

"That is probably true," she answered, "but that is because they live in darkness and their eyes are not accustomed to the bright light of the truth. They are like certain birds who can see in the dark but are

So if one can't see this, his government is off. ★

blinded in the daytime. What governs them is not the order of the world but their own desires, and so they think that the freedom to do wicked things and get away with them is a happy thing. But look at what the universal laws decree. Suppose that you have devoted your mind to higher things. You would not then need a judge to give you some kind of prize. It is you yourself who have achieved this excellent state. And suppose you turn to the bad. You don't need someone else to say that this must be punished, because you have done this to yourself. Think of it this way: you can look up at the blue sky and then down at the dirt; everything else in sight disappears and you feel yourself to be now down in the dirt and now up in the stars. Ordinary people don't look up at the stars. But does that mean that we have to join them, especially after we have concluded that they are like animals? Or suppose that you have a man who went completely blind, forgot that he had ever been able to see, and believed that he lacked nothing at all that pertains to human perfection. We, who do see, would not agree with him, would we? So when it comes down to something as fundamental as this, ordinary men will not concede that those who commit injustice are unhappier than those who suffer from what they have done."

"I'd like to hear your explanation of that proposition."

"You concede that every wicked man deserves punishment."

"Of course."

"And it is obvious that the wicked are in many ways unhappy."

"Yes, we have agreed about that."

"And you agree that those who deserve punishment are miserable?"

"Yes, I agree to that."

"Now, if you were a judge, which would you think should be punished, the one who has committed a crime or the one who suffered from it and was the victim?"

"The criminal, of course, should be punished and the victim should be compensated."

"So the criminal would be more miserable than the victim."

"That's true," I admitted.

"And by the same reasoning, it would follow that if dishonesty makes men miserable by its very nature, then an injustice that one man commits against another means misery for the perpetrator rather than for the victim."

"Yes, that's right."

"But lawyers are always arguing the opposite these days. They try to get judges to show mercy to the victims of crimes for their terrible injuries when, in fact, the mercy should be shown to the criminals.

Those who have done wrong should not be prosecuted with outrage and anger, but should be treated with kindness and sympathy, as if they were sick men who could have their guilt lessened by punishment, as if it were some kind of malignancy. This way, defense lawyers would have nothing to do, or, if they wanted to do men good, they would become prosecutors. And the criminals, if they could glimpse through some peephole at the virtue they had abandoned and if they could realize that, through their torments, they could lay aside the burden of their filthy vices, they would not think of them as torments but as cures. In their desire to acquire goodness they would reject any efforts of their advocates and give themselves over to the prosecutors and the judges. That is why, in the hearts of the wise, there should be no room for hatred. Only a fool would hate good men; and as for the bad, there is no reason to hate them either. Weakness is a disease of the body, and similarly wickedness is a disease of the mind. We feel sympathy rather than hatred for those who are sick, and those who suffer from a disability greater than any physical ailment deserve pity rather than blame."

Why do you work yourself up to excite the
    passions,
      and think of ways of committing suicide?

That death you so much long for is on its way
    of her own accord, drawn by her flying horses.
Men are the prey of serpents, lions, tigers,
    bears, and boars, with their sharp teeth and
        their claws,
and of other men, too, with glittering swords in
    their hands.

    Why should men hunt men? Because they are
      different?
Is that a reason to kill and be willing to die?
    The explanations they give are cruel but flimsy.
They are fools and cannot think or help
    themselves.
    Therefore love the good, and pity the wicked.

V

After a few moments, I ventured to remark, "Yes, I do understand what you are saying about the consequences that come to good men and to bad. Still, there is the popular idea of fortune. And no wise man, I think, would prefer poverty, disgrace, and exile to the alternative of remaining at home, powerful, prosperous, and respected. This is how wisdom can be seen to work—when the happiness of the rulers is passed on to the people they govern, especially if prisons and executions and all the other torments the law imposes are kept only for the wicked for whom they were intended. It surprises me that these things are turned upside down so that good men are oppressed by punishments that should have been given to criminals and bad men get rewards that should have gone to the virtuous. Can you explain to me how this confusion happens? I should be less puzzled if I could suppose that it was all aleatory and random. But my belief in God the ruler makes this hard to accept and deepens my confusion. God gives rewards to the just and punishments to the unjust, but he also seems to give delights to the wicked and harsh treatment to the good. Why should this be? And how is it different from pure chance?"

"If the true causes of something are not understood," she replied, "it can appear to be random and confused. But although you cannot understand the way things are ordered in the universe, you can rest assured that a good governor does indeed keep order and has a plan. You should not doubt that everything happens as it should."

Candide

One who has no idea of how Arcturus'
    post at the pole of heaven is constant
or how Boötes follows behind his wagon
    and descends so slowly into the sea,
although he springs up in the sky with alacrity,
    will be befuddled by heaven's motions.

The full moon grows dim in the earth's shadow
    and the stars turn away their faces,
and the men in the streets are afraid and bang
      their gongs
    in fear of what these events portend.
That the north wind blows the sea that beats on
      the rocks
    in wave after furious rumbling wave
is not surprising, nor that Phoebus' warmth
    can melt the snows in springtime
as everyone understands, for the causes are clear;
    other happenings, more obscure,
disturb the ignorant, fearful crowd, but give them
    knowledge and their faint hearts would be
      soothed.

VI

"Fine," I said, "but it is a part of our business for you to reveal these mysteries and explain those things that are clouded and hidden. I am disturbed by these inconsistencies and beg you to explain a little more fully the apparent randomness of good and bad fortune."

She hesitated a moment, then smiled, and at last replied, "This is the great question, isn't it? It is a problem that can never be fully solved even by the most exhaustive discourse. When one part of the conundrum is resolved, others pop up, like the heads of the Hydra. What is needed to restrain them is intellectual fire. Otherwise, we are in a morass of difficulties—the singleness of providence, the vicissitudes of fate, the haphazardness of events, God's plan, predestination, free will. All these knotty questions come together and are intertwined. But your cure depends in part on your knowledge of these matters, and, within the constraints of our time, I shall try to explain some of the fundamentals. If the delights of harmony and song gratify you, you must be patient for a bit while I construct the arguments and lay them out for you in proper sequence."

"However you want to do it," I replied.

Then, as if she were starting at the beginning, she spoke as follows. "The generation of all things and the development of things that change and move take their order and forms and causes from the unchangeable mind of God. That mind, in the lofty fortress of its oneness, set up the manner in which the multiplicity of things behave. This plan, when we think of it as the purity of God's understanding, we call providence. But when we think of it in reference to all the things in motion that it controls, we call it fate. And if you look at these two things and examine their meaning, you will see that they are different. Providence is divine reason itself, established by the highest ruler of all things, the reason that orders everything that exists. But fate is the disposition that is inherent in each of these things, through which providence binds all things together, each in its proper order. Providence embraces all things together, even though they are infinite in number and different from one another; but fate arranges the motions of separate things, distributed in various places, forms, and times. The unfolding of the order of time is united in the foresight of the mind of God, but that unity when distributed among things in the unfolding of time is what the ancients called fate.

"Now, while these are different, one depends on the other, for the order of fate comes from the simplicity of providence. Think of the way a craftsman imagines the form of the object he is about to make and then produces by many steps the thing he had planned in his mind and had thought of in an instant. In the same way, God's unchanging plan for what is to be done is providence, but it is by fate that he accomplishes these things in the course of time and step by step. And whether fate works by divine spirits that are the servants of providence, or is woven into the soul, or into the whole of nature, or is somehow a result of the movements of the stars, or is the consequence of the exertions of angels and demons, or some or all of these, it is certainly clear that the simple and unchanging plan of what happens is providence, and that fate is the intricate, moveable, interconnected, and temporal working out of these things according to the divine plan of what is to be done.

"It works out, then, that all things that are subject to fate are also subject to providence—to which fate is subordinate. Some things are immovable and fixed, ordered by providence directly, and above the course of fate. These are things that are close to God and beyond the realm of fate's movable nature. Think of a number of spheres revolving about a central point: the innermost sphere is a kind of pivot for the rest and it has the simplicity of centrality, moving the least, while those farther out move more, traveling over a greater circumference and separated from the immovability and indivisibility of the central point. Anything located at the center is less movable. Those things that are farther out and further separated from the divine mind are more subject to the complications of fate. As a thing gets closer to the center, it is less and less subject to fate. If it reaches the center, it is not subject to fate at all but it clings to the divine mind, which is motionless and above the vicissitudes of fate. So, as reasoning is to understanding, and as becoming is to being, and as time is to eternity, or the circle is to its center, so is the motion of fate to the unmoving simplicity of providence. It is providence that orders the motions of the stars, arranges the elements of matter with one another in proper proportion, and changes them in predictable ways. It renews the species of living things that are born and die through the growth of their offspring in their likeness, and it also orders the actions and the fortunes of men in an unbreakable chain of causes and effects, which arise from providence and must therefore be immutable. The best kind of government is the inflexible order of causes arising from the simplicity of the mind of God, so its immutability constrains what would otherwise be mutable and in flux.

"It may seem to you to be confused and confusing, but that is because you do not understand the underlying order. Still, the tendency that disposes all things toward the good is what directs them. Nothing happens for the sake of evil, even by the actions of the wicked themselves. They are seeking the good but are erroneous in their quest and have strayed from the correct path. Still, you ask why it should be that things come out unfairly—that for the good there can be both good and bad outcomes and for the bad, too, there can be both good and bad things that happen to them. But ask yourself whether these good and bad things must necessarily be as men judge them to be. The judgments of men conflict, after all, and there are some whom men think deserving of reward while others think them deserving of punishment.

"But let us suppose that there is someone who can accurately tell the difference between good and evil. Would even he be able to judge the inner temper (if we may borrow a term from physics) of men's minds? Your puzzlement is like that of a man who cannot figure out why, with healthy bodies, one person will like sweet things and another will prefer bitter things. It is true of the sick that some benefit from mild medicines while others require more drastic remedies—but the doctor is experienced with this kind of thing and is less puzzled by it. Now, what do you suppose characterizes the health of minds but goodness, or the sickness of minds but evil? And who else is the preserver of good things and the remover of evil things but God, the ruler and healer of minds? He looks down from his high fortress of providence, sees what is appropriate for each person, and arranges what he knows is fitting. This is where the marvelous machinery of fate comes into it, when he who knows does things that the ignorant cannot fathom.

"Let us consider a few examples of the depths of

God that are understandable by men. Take someone you think to be most just and honorable, although God knows that the opposite is true. Lucan, one of my protégés, tells us in the first book of the *Pharsalia* that in the struggle between Pompey and Caesar, God was of course on the winning side but Cato, whom everyone supposed to be a model of virtue, supported the losing side. So when you see something happen that is the opposite of what you might expect, it may be that you are wrong in your perceptions and that your thinking is confused, but there is order nonetheless in the way the events turn out. But let us go further and suppose there is someone so wise as to be able to hold the same judgments that God does, but he is weak in fortitude and strength of mind. If anything bad happens to him, he may waver in his belief because he has not been able to preserve his good fortune. A wise dispensation might well spare him because he is not suited to adversity, which will only make him worse. But now think of a better man, a holier man who is near to God and firmer in his belief. Providence does not allow someone like that to meet with any adversity, not even bodily illness. As somebody once said, 'The body of the holy man was constructed in heaven.'

"It can happen that supreme power is given to good men to check the power of the wicked. Others may receive a mixture of good and bad fortune according to the qualities of their minds. Providence will harass some because otherwise they might run to excess with unbroken prosperity. To others it may bring hardships in order to strengthen their minds with the qualities of piety and patience. Some people are very much afraid of suffering, which, as it turns out, they can bear as well as anyone else. Others are scornful of suffering, which in fact they cannot bear at all. To both kinds of error, providence brings correction and self-knowledge through suffering. Some men have won fame at the price of a glorious death. Some have suffered tortures and shown the world by their martyrdom that evil cannot triumph over good. It is right that these things happen, and we cannot question whether they are planned or properly suited to those to whom they happen.

"The wicked, too, have their moments of prosperity and of hardship, and these come from the same causes. No one finds it remarkable that they are sometimes punished, which is what we would expect. Their sufferings after all may deter others from crime even as they correct those who suffer. It is their good fortune that some good men find difficult to comprehend, and it does happen often enough. But I believe that this is planned also, for there could well be a person so impulsive and reckless that poverty may very well prompt him to steal. And for his weakness providence provides this remedy, giving him money so as to keep him from temptation. It can also happen that a wicked man whose conscience troubles him for his many misdeeds and who compares his comfortable state with the suffering he deserves may reform, so as not to lose his good fortune, leaving his wickedness behind him. Others, who have used their wealth and prosperity badly, are suddenly cast down into the catastrophe they deserve. And there are some bad men to whom the right to judge is given, so that they may be a kind of test for the good as well as the punishment for the wicked. There is no conspiracy among bad people, after all, and they do not agree among themselves. How could they, when each has vices tearing at his conscience and each often does things he later regrets having done?

"It can even come about through providence that evil men can make other evil men good, which is wonderful to contemplate. Some suffer injuries from others who they know are even worse, are filled with hatred of those who have hurt them, and have then returned to the side of goodness in an effort to be as unlike the objects of their hatred as possible. In God's mind, even evils can have good uses, and by their careful application God can contrive a good result. There is an ultimate order that governs all things, and when a thing has departed from this order it only falls into another category where a different order applies, but it is nonetheless order. So nothing governed by providence is left to chance.

"But it is not right that I should be speaking as if I were a god. God is beyond human comprehension and his powers cannot be expressed in words. It is enough to have understood only this: that God is the author of all natures, orders all things and directs them toward the good. He holds all creation in his own image and, by a chain of necessity that fate presides over, he banishes evil from his domain. So if you could see the way providence disposes of all things that are spread over the earth, you would be able to judge that there is no evil in any of them. But this has gone on for a long while, and I see that you are tired. What you need is some relief in the charms of poetry. I offer you a refreshing drink so that you will be able to concentrate when we continue our reasoning.

If you would see with your mind's eye
the laws of the mind of the most high God,
look up at the stars that wheel in the heavens
in peace in their intricate elegant courses.
The sun with his ruddy fire does not

delay Phoebe's colder car
of the moon, nor does the dancing Bear
follow the other stars to set
below the ocean's distant edge.
Instead he remains at his polar post.
At balanced times the evening star
announces the coming of night, while the
     morning
star declares the return of the light.
Their motions are all expressions of love,
for there is no strife in those celestial
regions above us, but rather concord
regulating the conversation
of wet with dry and of hot with cold.
Flames leap up, while the heavy earth
presses downward: thus they dance.
The warmth of springtime calls forth blooming
flowers that perfume the air;
hot summer dries the grain in the fields;
autumn brings the happy harvest;
and in wintertime the rains come down
to nourish and refresh the earth.
These delicate balances order all
that live and breathe on the bountiful earth,
and that same order takes them away
at the end, when their span of time has run.
But always above there sits the Lord

who rules all things and holds in his hands
the reins that guide his whole creation,
the ruler, the *fons et origo.*
The lawgiver, the wise judge,
he stirs the stars and planets to motion
and yet controls their paths and orbits,
lest they run wild to break from their circles,
tearing the sky into pieces reducing
the universe to its building blocks,
but the bonds of love hold those pieces in place,
love for each other and love of the good
that is their aim and only end.
How else could the firmament stay firm
unless the love that gave it a start
did not flow back in grateful return?

Beauty

VII

"Now, do you see where all our talk has been leading?"

"Where is that?" I asked.

"What we have been saying is that every kind of fortune is good."

"But how is that possible?" I asked.

"Consider this. Every kind of fortune, whether pleasing or painful, is granted to men for the purpose of rewarding or testing good men, or else of punishing or correcting those who are bad. Every kind of fortune is good, then, because it is just or useful."

"I see the logic of that," I admitted. "And if I think about providence, of which you spoke a while ago, or fate, I see how your argument is well founded. But it is also, if I may say, absurd on its face."

"How so?"

"People say all the time that this man or that is unfortunate. That he has bad fortune."

"You want us to use words that the common people do so as to avoid the appearance of having moved too far from common sense?"

"If you could, yes," I said.

"Do you think that something that is useful and profitable is good?"

"Yes, of course."

"And whatever disciplines or corrects is useful?"

"Yes, it would be."

"And therefore good?"

"Yes."

"Now, this kind of fortune is either for men who are on virtue's path and who have to battle with adversity, or for those who, after quitting their wickedness, turn to virtue and goodness."

"I suppose so, yes."

"What do you think about good fortune that is given to the virtuous as a reward? You have no objection to that, do you?"

"No, that's a good thing, as all men agree."

"And bad fortune that punishes the wicked? Do people think this is a good thing?"

"No, they don't. They think it's the worst thing imaginable."

"Aha! You see what a curious conclusion we have arrived at by following the opinion of the common people."

"What is that?" I asked.

"Well it would seem from the premises that have been granted, that for those who are virtuous, or making progress toward virtue, whatever fortune comes to them is good. But for those who are persevering in their wickedness, every kind of fortune is bad."

"That's where the logic leads, although few people would be comfortable admitting it."

"So a wise man experiencing bad fortune ought not to take it badly, in the same way that a brave man should not object to the sounds of war trumpets blaring. For each of these, after all, the obstacle is the occasion for their kinds of excellence, the latter to increase his glory and the former to refine his wisdom. And this is why virtue—*virtus,* which can also

mean strength or vigor—is called by that name, because it relies on its own powers and is not undone
by adversity. After all, you are set on the path to virtue, and you are not wallowing in luxury or lolling in
sybaritic pleasures. You are engaged in mental strug-
gles lest bad fortune oppress you or good fortune
corrupt you and make you soft. Whoever falls short
or exceeds what is normal holds happiness in contempt and is not rewarded for his efforts. The kind
of fortune you want to fashion for yourself is up to
you. All fortune that may seem adverse, if it does not
test you, punishes."

For ten long years, Agamemnon struggled at Troy
to avenge the insult to his brother's marriage bed.
When his fleet had been becalmed at Aulis he
    paid
the gods of the winds with his daughter's precious
    blood,
stern king then rather than grieving father,
and they cut her innocent throat. The Ithacan,
    too,
wept for his lost comrades whom Polyphemus,
the one-eyed Cyclops, had grabbed and gobbled
    up,
and his bitter tears were in the end rewarded.
Hercules' fame came from his arduous labors:

he tamed the Centaurs, bested the Nemean lion,
shot the Stymphalian birds with his sharp arrows,
snatched the Hesperides' apples from the
     watchful
dragon, put a leash on Cerberus' heads,
and captured Diomedes' dreadful mares,
whose fodder was human flesh, and fed them
     their master.
He managed to kill the many-headed Hydra,
and broke the horn of Acheloüs, the god
of the river who took the shape of an ox and,
     shamed,
hid his wound in the sands of the riverbank.
He wrestled with the Lybian king, Antaeus,
and pinned him on the sand. Cacus, too,
who rustled the cattle, Hercules caught and
     killed.
He hunted down the Erymanthian boar
and bore the weight of the sky on his broad
     shoulders.
For that last labor, heaven granted him
his great reward. You, too, should follow his steep
path, learn from his example, take
courage and struggle onward. Never falter
in laziness or fear, but overcome
the earth's trials and ascend to the stars' heights.

BOOK V

I

She had finished her recitation and was about to broach another subject, when I spoke up and said, "You have discoursed well and authoritatively about providence and how it is related to many other issues, which I can attest to from my own experience. But it occurs to me to ask you whether you find any room at all in your theories for the operation of pure chance. Is there such a thing? And, if so, what is it?"

"I am trying to get you home," she said, "and while that is an interesting question and well worth exploring, I am afraid that if we wander down every appealing byway, you may not have the endurance to reach our goal. I should recommend that we take the most direct route."

"You needn't doubt my energy or my interest," I answered. "Don't worry about me. I'm sure I shall be able to find a resting place somewhere along the way. But the question is a fascinating one and I delight in your explanations. I am sure I shall find whatever you tell me credible. I am unlikely to have doubts or raise objections."

"Very well, then, I shall do as you ask," she said, and she addressed the topic I had asked her to discuss. "If chance is defined as events produced by random motions rather than by a chain of causes, then I should assert that chance is nothing at all. I should even say that, apart from being what we are talking about, it is a word entirely devoid of meaning. If God controls all things in his ordering, what room is left for the operation of chance? It is an obvious truth that nothing comes from nothing, and none of the ancients ever took issue with that view. Rather, they accepted it as a fundamental premise of their thinking about nature, even though they applied it not so much to the creative principle as to the material world that it produced. But if something were to arise from no cause at all, it could be said to have come from nothing—which can't possibly be, which in turn means that chance, as we have defined it, cannot exist."

"Is there nothing at all that can be called fortuitous? Isn't there anything to which the word 'chance' pertains?"

"Aristotle offers a meaning in his *Physics* that seems to me to make sense."

"And what did he say?"

"Whenever something is done for the sake of some

particular purpose and something else occurs, different from what was intended, it is called 'chance.' For instance, if a man were digging in the ground in order to plant something in his field and he found a buried sack of gold, this would be what people call chance. But on the other hand, it wouldn't have come from nothing. There were causes, although their unforeseen and unexpected results would have appeared to produce a chance event. If the man had not been digging in the ground, and if the man who had hidden the gold had not buried it in that particular spot, the gold would not have been found. These are the causes of that lucky profit, produced by the two causes coming together, although not by the intention of either man. Neither the man who hid the gold nor the man digging in the field intended that the gold should be found. But there was a coincidence in that one man happened to be digging where the other had hidden his treasure. We can define chance, then, as the unexpected result of causes that come together of things that were done for some other purpose. Now, the confluence of these causes and their connection derives from providence, which disposes of all things in their appropriate times and places."

Under the distant Persian cliffs where the
Parthian bowmen

turned in their flight to shoot at pursuing
hordes,
the Tigris and the Euphrates arise from a single
source,
but separate their courses, dividing their
waters;
and yet, if they came together, the river craft
making their way
would meet, as would tree trunks torn up by
the flood
in the waters that swirled together into their
random path.
But would it be random? The contour of the
ground
and the way water flows downward, seeking its
level,
are predetermined, so that slack-reined
chance
could be shown in the end to be wearing its own
bridle of laws
that all along governed its every movement.

II

"I can follow your logic and I understand what you
are saying, but in all this closely linked series of
causes, is there no room for free will? Or does the

chain of providence also constrain the motions of men's minds?"

"Oh, there is freedom," she replied, "for otherwise there could not be any rational nature. Rational beings must possess freedom of the will. Those beings that are rational have the faculty of judgment by which reason operates and decides everything. On its own, then, it distinguishes which things are to be avoided from those to be desired. And what a man judges to be desirable is what he seeks, while he flees what he judges to be undesirable. So it follows that those who have reason have freedom to will or not to will, although this freedom is not equal in all of them. Celestial and divine beings have clearer judgments, an uncorrupted will, and the ability to achieve what they seek. And human souls are more free when they persevere in the contemplation of the mind of God, less free when they descend to the corporeal, and even less free when they are entirely imprisoned in earthly flesh and blood. Their ultimate enslavement is when they give themselves up to vice and no longer exercise their powers of reason. They have lowered their eyes from the highest truth to dark, base things and are wrapped in a cloud of ignorance. They give in to destructive whims and consent to those things that strengthen their bonds of slavery. They have brought this upon themselves and are therefore captives of their exercise of their innate freedom. But still, providence looks after them from eternity, sees what they do, and disposes rewards and punishments according to what each person has deserved."

Homer sings of how Phoebus' light
"sees all things and hears all things,"*
but his rays are not strong enough to pierce
to the inmost depths of earth and sea.
But this is not so for the great Creator,
whose gaze goes deeper, unobstructed
by matter's opacity or night's
utter blackness. Instead, he sees
what is, what was, and what is to come
in an instant's insight—only his,
who is the true and only sun.

III

"I am still confused," I confessed. "I have another and perhaps even more difficult question."

"And what is that?" she asked. "I have some idea already about what may be troubling you."

"I don't see how God can have foreknowledge of

---

* Homer *Iliad* 3.227.

everything and that there can still be free will. If God sees everything that will happen, and if he cannot be mistaken, then what he foresees must necessarily happen. And if he knows from the very beginning what all eternity will bring, not only men's actions but their thoughts and desires will be known to him, and that means that there cannot be any free will. There couldn't be any thought or action that divine providence, which is never mistaken, did not know about in advance. If anyone deviated from what was planned, then there would have been no foreknowledge of the future, but only a guess, an uncertain opinion, which is not what any pious person could suppose that God would have.

"I have heard all kinds of arguments by which people try to solve this conundrum, but I am not persuaded by any of them. They say, for instance, that a thing cannot happen because providence foresees that it will, but rather that since something is going to be, providence has foreseen it, which just puts necessity on the other side but leaves it still in operation. They say that it is not necessary that foreseen things will happen, but that things that will happen are foreseen. All this does is change the subject to the question of which is the cause of which— foreknowledge of the necessity of future events, or future events being known to providence. Whichever way you come down, this was not the question we were addressing. And in any event, it leaves us with the idea that, for whatever cause, the outcome of future events is known in advance, and therefore the question remains as to how foreknowledge does not confer on an event the necessity of happening.

"Say that someone sits down. Anyone who has the opinion that that person is sitting must be correct. And on the other hand, if the opinion is true, then the person must be sitting. There is a necessity either way. In the latter, he must be sitting, and in the former the opinion is correct. But who would say that the man is sitting because the opinion is correct? The sitting happened first. Thus, although the cause of the truth flows one way, there is a common necessity on both sides.

"The same logic applies to providence and future events. Even if they are foreseen because they are future events, they do not occur because they are foreseen. Still, either things must be foreseen by God because they are coming, or they must come because they are foreseen. That is enough, all by itself, to make free will impossible. And yet, how topsy-turvy it is, after all, to say that the cause of divine foreknowledge is the occurrence of temporal events. But what other inference are we to draw from that idea that God foresees events because they are destined to happen except to suppose that those things, once they have happened, are the source of his foreknowledge? When I know that something is, it is necessary that it be so, and in the same way, when I know that something is going to happen, then it is necessary that it shall happen. The occurrence of an event that is foreknown cannot be avoided.

"And finally, if anyone thinks that something is different from what it really is, then that is not knowledge but a false opinion, and wrong. So if something is destined to happen in a way that cannot be foretold and is not certain, who could have foreknowledge of it? Just as real knowledge is unmixed with falsity, so it is that something correctly known cannot be otherwise than it is known to be. The reason that there is not any deception in knowledge is that it is necessary for things to be exactly as knowledge understands them to be. The question, then, is how God can know in advance that these things will happen if they are uncertain. If he thinks that they will certainly happen even though there is some possibility that they won't, then he is mistaken, which is outrageous and even wicked to think or say. On the other hand, if he knows that they may or may not happen, what kind of knowledge is that? Then he doesn't actually know anything! How is that different from what Horace has Tiresias say in one of his satires: 'Whatever I say will happen, or maybe not'?* How is God's divine foreknowledge different from mere opinion if, like men, he considers things that are uncertain? If the mind of God cannot be uncertain, then those things that he knows will happen absolutely must happen. And if that is true, then human thoughts and actions have no freedom about them at all, because the mind of God sees all things in advance and can never be led astray, which means that his certainty compels all thoughts and actions to happen.

"We have to conclude then that there is no freedom in human actions or even intentions, and that the mind of God, foreseeing everything without mistakes or uncertainties, constrains all things to come to pass. And once we have accepted this, all human affairs turn out to be nothing like what we have supposed, for there cannot be punishments for evil or rewards for good if there are no free and voluntary actions on anybody's part. What we judge to be just turns out to be most unjust, because to punish the wicked for what they couldn't help, or indeed to reward the good for deeds over which they had no control, makes no sense at all. There are no virtues and no vices anymore, but only a jumble of rewards

---

* Horace *Satires* 2.5.59.

and punishments of merits and faults that cannot be distinguished from one another. What could be more pernicious than the ordering of all things from providence and the irrelevance of all human intentions? It would follow that even our vices are the responsibility of the Creator of all things that are good. It would also mean that there is no sense in hoping or praying for something good to happen or for something evil to be averted. What would be the point of hopes or prayers if all events are fixed in an inflexible pattern that cannot change in any way?

"The consequence of that would be that the main basis of conversation between men and God would be removed, for even with the proper humility and the inestimable favor of God's grace, there is nothing that he can do for us, no help he can offer, no relief. Our supplications are pointless and irrelevant, and it is mostly through our prayers that we can approach the remote light of the divine. But this connection is broken if we conclude that it is useless and we can no longer cling to him or feel ourselves joined in any way with the master of all being. So where would that leave us except, as you sang a while earlier, as a humanity, torn apart, and in decline toward weakness and exhaustion?"

What strife breaks the civil bonds
of the things of this world? What God would set

such incompatible truths loose
to struggle thus with one another?
Either could stand alone, but together
how can their contradictions be joined?
Or is there some way that they can get on
that the human mind, enmeshed in flesh,
cannot discern? That flame is covered,
and in the darkness the world's subtle
connections are hidden. And yet we feel
the warmth of the love that holds together
all that there is in eternal truth
that knows what it seeks and has its end
in its beginning. But which of us yearns
to learn those things he already knows?
And is that wisdom or is it blindness?
(And how do we know that we do not know
what we do not know?) If it were found,
could the ignorant seeker recognize it?
From our minds to the mind of God
is an awesome leap: the infinite number
of separate truths that are yet all one
leave us breathless. The body's dense
flesh obscures our recollection
of the separate truths and the one truth
and yet allows us at least to suspect
that we all live in an awkward state
with inklings of our ignorance
that turn out to be our greatest wisdom—

as if we had long ago ascended
and beheld from on high the exalted vision
of which we now retain nothing
but the sense of loss of that exaltation.

IV

Then she said, "This is that old conundrum about providence that Cicero talked about in *On Divination*, and you have just gone into it at some length. But no one has scrutinized the question with sufficient rigor, and the reason that the problem is difficult is that the operation of reason in the human mind cannot approach the workings of the mind of God or understand the immediacy of divine prescience. If this immediacy could be somehow understood, then all the difficulties would be resolved. I shall try to explain some of this a little later on, but first we have to deal with those issues that are troubling you right now. You don't feel comfortable about those explanations of how foreknowledge does not imply predestination or restrict the operation of free will. You have not produced any proof of predestination except the logical quirk that those things that are known in advance cannot not happen. But if foreknowledge did not impose any predestination on futurity, would acts of will be predestined?"

"No."

"So let us say that there is foreknowledge but that it does not impose predestination. In that case, freedom of the will would remain absolute. And here you might object that even if foreknowledge is not the same as predestination, it is a sign that the future will happen inevitably in a certain way. And in that case, even without foreknowledge, we could all agree that the future is predestined, since signs may point to what exists but do not cause those things that they signify. So you would have to demonstrate first that nothing can happen that is not predestined and that foreknowledge is a sign of that necessity. Otherwise, if there is no predestination, then the foreknowledge cannot be a sign of something that does not exist. We know that we cannot deduce a proof from signs or from external arguments that are outside the subject. We have to limit ourselves to arguments that are coherent and that fit together and lead from one proposition to the next.

"It is impossible that what is foreseen does not come to pass. It would mean that events that the mind of God could foretell did not then happen, or the alternative would be to believe that although they happen, they were not predestined by their own nature. You can understand it in this way: we look at many things as they are happening, like charioteers in a race, for example. But there is no necessity in the outcome, is there, or in any of the things that happen during the race?"

"No, because then the exercise of skill would be beside the point."

"So anything that happens without necessity or predestination is, before it happens, a future event about to happen but not by necessity. There are, then, some things that are going to happen that are not compelled by necessity. Just as the knowledge of things that are happening in the present imposes no necessity on what will happen next, so too foreknowledge imposes no necessity on what is about to happen. That, of course, is at the very heart of the question, as I'm sure you are about to say—whether there can be any foreknowledge of things that are not inevitable. There appears to be a contradiction here, and you think that the inevitability of events is a consequence of their being known in advance, while if there is no inevitability, then they cannot be known in advance—because nothing can be known unless it is sure and certain. If an event that is foreseen is uncertain, then the foreknowledge of it is only an opinion, a guess, not the certainty of knowledge of the truth. To have opinions about something that turns out to be different in fact from what you thought is not the same as having knowledge about it.

The reason for this mistake is that people assume that the limit of their knowledge depends on the capacity to be known of the objects of knowledge. But this is wrong. Things that are known are not comprehended according to how knowable they are by nature but rather according to the ability to know of those who are doing the knowing. Take for instance a sphere, which is recognizable both by sight and by touch. The one who sees it can be at a distance and he sees it all at once by the rays of light that pass from the eye. The one who touches it has to come close, grasp it, and sense its roundness piece by piece. In the same way, man is perceived in different ways—by sense perception, imagination, reason, and intuitive intellect. The senses perceive his shape as made up of matter, while imagination considers his shape without paying attention to matter. Reason then transcends imagination and with a universal consideration looks at the specific form itself of each individual. The point of view of intuitive intellect is higher still, for instead of passing around a man from different angles, piece by piece, it takes in all at once with the mind's eye focused on the thing itself. And this is what you must understand, that the higher powers of comprehension embrace and include those that are lower, while the lower do not rise to include the higher. Sense cannot perceive anything

The ability of the knower to know

beyond the material. Imagination does not take into account the universal forms. Reason does not comprehend individual forms. The intuitive intelligence, however, as if it were looking down from a lofty vantage point, perceives the universal form and distinguishes all things that partake of it—but in a way that allows it to understand the form itself, which cannot be known in any other way. It includes the reason's theoretical understading, and the imagination's shape, and the senses' materiality, but it is not by the use of reason, imagination, and the senses, but rather by a single stroke of the mind, taking in all these aspects together and at once.

"Reason, when it looks at something without using imagination or the senses, grasps the imaginable and sensible aspects, because reason is what defines the universal. Reason tells us, for example, that man is a rational two-legged animal. But when we hear this, we do not suppose that man is not also an imaginable and sensible being that reason is considering and describing, using its capabilities rather than those of imagination or sense perception. In the same way, imagination, although it starts out with information from the senses, nonetheless goes beyond sense perception and surveys all sensible things not by the information of the sense organs but in an imaginative way. So you may understand from this

OK!

that all ways of knowing use their own capacity and capability rather than depending on the object that is being known. And this makes sense because every act of judgment involves the one judging, whose powers are his own rather than those of the thing or person being judged."

On the philosophers' painted stoa
the ancient thinkers instructed
how it can happen that we
perceive in the outside world
images of those objects
that then appear in our minds.
So does the sharp stylus
incise on the blank wax
untouched by thoughts or words
the meaning the writer intends.
Is the mind like that empty page,
featureless and passive,
or like a polished mirror
that reflects what comes before it?
How can we speak of the keenness
of a person's mind or the power
to analyze a problem,
breaking it down into parts
or putting those parts together?
How can it lift itself

to the loftiest of ideas
or descend to the sordid depths?
It can turn upon itself
and allow the false to refute
and overthrow the truth.
 Forceful it is, and active,
and it does not merely submit
to the imprint of outside things,
but on its own it stirs
and moves by its own powers,
as when light strikes the eyes
or voices sound in the ears.
The mind, then roused, calls forth
forms that are waiting within it
to make their similar motions,
and these refine and combine
with the marks received from outside
to produce by their intercourse
the offspring we know as thoughts.

V

"So where we are is that in perceiving corporeal
things, even though the stimuli from outside affect
the senses, and the forms in the mind are summoned
up from where they lie at rest, the mind makes its

judgments as well as it can. But consider the case of
beings that are not corporeal and are free from all
such influences. They can rouse the mind to activity
without the need of external stimuli for perceptions.
On this principle, there are many kinds of knowledge that various creatures have. Living creatures
that do not move—oysters and clams, for example—
cling to rocks and feed, and they have sense perception. But other creatures that move, pursuing prey or
evading predators, have imagination as well, which
prompts them to move this way or that. Reason belongs only to humans, as intuitive intellect belongs
only to the mind of God. It follows then that this last
is the highest kind of knowledge, for its scope includes that of all the others and goes beyond them.

"But let us suppose that sense and imagination
were to contradict reason and declare that what the
universal reason believes it has perceived is nothing
at all. What is available to sense and imagination
cannot be the universal, after all, and therefore either the judgment of reason is correct (in which case
there is nothing sensible) or else, since many things
are perceptible by the senses and imagination, reason's reports are unreliable, because she interprets
evidence of the senses and the imagination as if it
were a kind of universal. And now let us suppose
that reason's answer is that she sees both the evi-

dence of the senses and of the imagination but also sees their universality, but, as she goes on to say, neither sense nor imagination is capable of going beyond their reports of corporeal shapes. Must we not then rely on the judgments of reason as being the more nearly perfect way of knowing things? We have reason, after all, and we can understand that kind of claim and would have to agree with it. It is much like that when we look at the difference between human reason and divine intelligence. Human reason cannot understand how divine intelligence can see future events except in the same way that humans see them. And that is what you have been arguing, is it not? If things seem not to have certain and necessary outcomes, then you suppose they cannot be foreknown as being about to happen. Therefore, you think that there is no foreknowledge, but if there were foreknowledge there could be nothing that happened except from necessity. We have a share of reason. But if we could go beyond that to a share of divine knowledge, then, just as we have judged that reason is superior to sense data and information, so you would find that divine knowledge is superior to reason. Suppose that we could be raised up to participate in that divine knowledge. There, reason would comprehend what it cannot understand on her own.

Fides et
Ratio

And one of the things reason would understand would be how even those things that do not have a definite and certain outcome can be nevertheless known by the mind of God in its simplicity and loftiness and unboundedness."

Existence of divine knowledge assumed / believed, then appealed to

How various, how rich are the kinds of living
    creatures
that wander the earth, dragging their length
    along in the dust,
or plowing the farmer's furrows, or beating the
    winds with their wings
to float above us at swim in the lovely liquid
    air!
Others tread the ground, leaving a trail of
    footprints
in meadows they cross or the deep woods in
    which they lurk.
But all these curious creatures with their diverse
    forms and habits
turn their faces downward, their senses confined
    and dull,
while only the race of men can hold their heads
    up high
and stand with upright bodies, lords of the earth
    they look down on.

Unless you, too, are drawn downward by the lures
of earth
and flesh, you may turn your face above and gaze
at heaven
as your body's posture allows and even commands
you to do,
letting your mind soar high, free of the earth's
mire
to the depths of which you can at any moment
sink back.

VI

"As we have agreed, I think, things are known not according to their natures but according to the nature
of the one who is comprehending them. Let us consider, then, insofar as we can, what the nature of divine substance must be so that we can have some in-
kling of the kind of knowledge the divine mind has.
All who live by reason agree that God is eternal, and
we must therefore think about what eternity means.
This will clarify what the divine nature is and also
what divine knowledge must be. Eternity is the
whole, simultaneous, perfect possession of limitless
life, which we can better understand perhaps by
comparing it to temporal things. One who lives in

Important line
Prem. 1

time progresses in the present from the past and into the future. There is nothing in time that can embrace the entirety of his existence. He has no idea about tomorrow and has already lost his hold on the past. In this day-to-day life, he lives only in the transitory moment. Whatever is in time—even though, as Aristotle says, time had no beginning and has no ending and extends into infinity—is still not what may correctly be called 'eternal.' Its life may be infinitely long, but still it does not comprehend its entire extent simultaneously. It is still waiting for the future to reveal itself and it has let go of much of the past. What may properly be called eternal is quite different, in that it has knowledge of the whole of life, can see the future, and has lost nothing of the past. It is in an eternal present and has an understanding of the entire flow of time.

P 2

"Those philosophers are wrong, then, who took Plato's dictum that the world had no beginning and had no end and inferred from that that the created world is co-eternal with the Creator. It is one thing to proceed through infinite time, as Plato posits, but quite another to embrace the whole of time in one simultaneous present. This is obviously a property of the mind of God. God should not be thought of as older than the created world but different in his grasp of time in the immediacy of his being. The

endless and infinite changing of things in time is an
attempt to imitate eternity, but it cannot equal its
immobility and it fails to achieve the eternal present,
producing only an infinite number of future and past
moments. It never ceases to be and therefore is an
imitation of eternity, but it is balanced on the knife-
edge of the present, the brief and fleeting instant,
which we may call a kind of costume of eternity. But
since it is not equal to that eternal state, it falls from
immobility to change, from the immediacy of a con-
tinuing present to the infinite extent of past and future moments, and it confers on whatever possesses
it the appearance of what it imitates. And since it
could not abide in permanence, it seized instead on
the infinite flow of time, an endless succession of
moments, and in that way could appear to have a
continuity, which is not the same as permanence. All
this is to say that if we use proper terms, then, following Plato, we should say that God is eternal but
the world is perpetual.

"Now, since every judgment is able to comprehend things only according to the nature of the mind
making that judgment, and since God has an eternal
and omnipresent nature, his knowledge surpasses
time's movements and is made in the simplicity of a
continual present, which embraces all the vistas of
the future and the past, and he considers all this in

the act of knowing as though all things were going on at once. This means that what you think of as his foreknowledge is really a knowledge of the instant, which is never-passing and never-coming-to-be. It is not pre-vision (*praevidentia*) but providence (*providentia*), because, from that high vantage point, he sees at once all things that were and are and are to come. You insist that those things of the future are inevitable if God can see them, but you must admit that not even men can make inevitable those things that they see. Your seeing them in the present does not confer any inevitability, does it?"

"No, not at all."

"And if you accept the distinction between the human and the divine present, then it would follow that, just as you see things in the temporal present, he must see things in the eternal present. So his divine prescience does not change the nature of things, but he sees them in his present time just as they will come to be in what we think of as the future. And he cannot be confused but sees and understands immediately all things that will come to pass whether they are necessitated or not—just as you can see at the same time a man walking on the ground and the sun rising in the sky, and, although the two sights coincide, you understand immediately that the man's walking is willed and the sun's rising is necessitated.

And it is similarly true that his observation does not affect the things he sees that are present to him but future in terms of the flow of time. And this means that his foresight is not opinion but knowledge based on truth and that he can know something is going to happen and at the same time be aware that it lacks necessity.

"Now, if you were to say that what God sees as going to occur cannot not occur and that what cannot not occur happens of necessity, and make a problem of the word 'necessity,' I will answer that it is absolutely true but is, indeed, a problem, not so much for logicians as for theologians. All I can tell you is that this future event from the point of view of divine knowledge is necessary, but from its own nature is utterly and entirely free. There are actually two necessities, one of them simple—as that all men are mortal—and the other conditional—as that when you see a man walking it is necessary that he be walking. Whatever you know cannot be otherwise than as you know it. But this conditional necessity is different from the simple kind in that it is not caused by the thing's nature but by the addition of the condition. It is not necessary that a man go for a walk, even though it is necessary, when he is walking, that he is walking. It is in the same way that if divine providence sees anything in its eternal present, that must necessarily be, even though there is no necessity in its nature. God can see as present future events that happen as a result of free will. Thus, they are, from God's point of view, necessary, although in themselves they do not lose the freedom that is in their nature. All those things, then, that God knows will come to be will, indeed, come to be, some of them proceeding from free will, so that when they come to be they will not have lost the freedom of their nature, according to which, until the time that they happened, they might not have happened. So why is it important that they are not necessary if, from the aspect of divine knowledge, it turns out that they are tantamount to being necessary? It is like the examples I proposed to you a moment ago of the rising sun and the walking man. While these things are happening, they cannot not be happening, but of the two, only one was bound to happen while the other was not. In the same way, the things God sees in his eternal present will certainly happen, but some will happen because of the necessity of things and others will happen because of those who are doing those actions. From the aspect of divine knowledge, then, they are necessary, but considered in themselves they are free from the compulsion of ne-

Yeah, this def. works

You need to look w/ 2 perspectives
1) As it is in itself
2) As it is in God's knowledge

cessity. So are things that you look at with the senses singular, but if you look at them from the point of view of reason, they are universal.

"And now you may perhaps object that it lies in your power to change your intention and thereby to frustrate providence and turn it into nonsense, because whatever providence may have foreseen, you can do something else. And my answer is that you can decide to do something else, but the truth of providence will have seen that as well in its eternal present, and whatever you may try to do that is different or unpredictable will have been understood and predicted, whichever way you turn, so that you cannot avoid or evade divine foreknowledge, just as you cannot escape being seen by an eye that is focused on you, even though you decide to dart one way when you had been going in another direction. And what would you reply? That it is within your power to alter divine knowledge, since you were going to do this but abruptly changed your mind and chose instead to do that, and therefore divine knowledge must have changed just as quickly? It is not at all the case. Divine prescience runs ahead of everything and recollects it to the eternal present of its own knowledge. It does not change because it does not need to, having already foreseen the change you made at the last moment. God has this complete knowledge and understanding and vision of all things not from the unfolding of the events themselves but from the simplicity of his own perfect knowledge. It is in this light that we can answer the question you posed a while back about our providing a part of God's knowledge. The power of his knowledge includes everything in an eternal present and does not at all rely on the unfolding of later events. In this way, man's freedom is maintained in its integrity, and therefore God's rewards and punishments are meted out fairly and appropriately, because free will is operating and men are not compelled by necessity. God has prescience and is a spectator from on high, and as he looks down in his eternal present, he assigns rewards to the good and punishments to the wicked. In this way, our hopes and our prayers are not at all in vain. Our prayers, if they are of the right kind and are pleasing to God, are not without effect. And the conclusion, then, is clear, that you must avoid wickedness and pursue the good. Lift up your mind in virtue and hope and, in humility, offer your prayers to the Lord. Do not be deceived. It is required of you that you do good and that you remember that you live in the constant sight of a judge who sees all things."